Fiona Venn is a lecturer in United States history at the University of Essex. She is the author of *Oil Diplomacy in the Twentieth Century* (1986), and at present is working on a short study of the New Deal.

Makers of the Twentieth Century

FRANKLIN D.
Roosevelt

FIONA VENN

CaRDÍNaL

A CARDINAL Book

First published in Great Britain in Cardinal by Sphere Books Ltd 1990

Copyright © Fiona Venn 1990

The photographs which appear on the inside
front and inside back cover of this book are
reproduced with the kind permission of Hulton
Picture Co.

Typeset by Leaper & Gard Ltd, Bristol
Printed and bound in Great Britain by
Cox & Wyman Ltd, Reading

ISBN 0 7474 0427 5

Sphere Books Ltd
A Division of
Macdonald & Co (Publishers) Ltd
Orbit House
1 New Fetter Lane
London EC4A 1AR
A member of Maxwell Macmillan Pergamon Publishing Corporation

The author and publishers wish to thank the following who have kindly given permission for the use of copyright material: W.H. Allen & Co. PLC for an extract from James Roosevelt (with Bill Liddy), *My Parents: A Differing View* (1977); André Deutsch Ltd for extract from Joseph P. Lash, *Eleanor and Franklin* (1972); Dodd, Mead and Company for an extract from Hugh Gregory Gallagher, *FDR's Splendid Deception* (1985); Harper and Row for extracts from William Leuchtenberg, *Franklin D. Roosevelt and the New Deal* (1963); Houghton Mifflin Company for extracts from Arthur M. Schlesinger Jr, *The Age of Roosevelt* (3 vols, 1956–60); Random House Inc. for extracts from Studs Terkel, *Hard Times: An Oral History of the Great Depression* (1970); Routledge & Kegan Paul for an extract from Paul Conkin, *The New Deal* (1968); The Viking Press for an extract from Frances Perkins, *The Roosevelt I Knew* (1947); Harcourt Brace Jovanovich for an extract from James MacGregor Burns, *Roosevelt: The Lion and the Fox 1882–1940* (1956); William Heinemann Ltd for an extract from Martin Gilbert, *Road to Victory: Winston S. Churchill 1941–1945* (1986); Little, Brown and Co. for an extract from Frank B. Freidel, *Franklin D. Roosevelt: The Triumph* (1956); Oxford University Press for an extract from Robert Dallek, *Franklin D. Roosevelt and American Foreign Policy 1932–1945* (1979); and Simon and Schuster for an extract from Ted Morgan, *FDR: A Biography* (1985).

Although every effort has been made to contact copyright holders of all material used in this book the publishers would be pleased to hear from any copyright holders whom we have been unable to trace if their material appears in this book.

Acknowledgements

I have incurred several debts in the preparation of this book. I am particularly grateful to the Franklin and Eleanor Roosevelt Foundation for research funding and to the staff of the Franklin D. Roosevelt Library, Hyde Park, New York, for their patience and assistance. A number of good friends and colleagues read sections of this book in manuscript and I have profited from their valuable suggestions; I especially thank Peter Boyle, Hugh Brogan, Richard Crockatt and Philip Hills. I owe a special debt to the editor of this series, John Campbell, for his support, advice and constructive criticism. Needless to say, I am entirely responsible for any errors or omissions which remain. My many students over the years have contributed to my interpretation of the New Deal and of Roosevelt's foreign policy, and I look forward to continuing the debate with their successors. Last, but not least, I thank my family: Tim for his unfailing encouragement, love and moral support; and my children, Elizabeth and Jonathan, for their forbearance and tolerant acceptance of my preoccupation. I dedicate this book to them, in the hope that it may be a partial compensation.

Fiona Venn
Colchester, January 1990

Contents

	Editor's Foreword	ix
	Chronology	xi
	Map of USA in 1933	xiv
1	The Early Life	1
2	The Governor of New York	17
3	The First New Deal, 1933–35	36
4	The Second New Deal, 1935–38	57
5	The Internationalist as Isolationist, 1933–41	78
6	Roosevelt the International Statesman, 1941–45	101
7	Conclusion	121
	Maps showing Electoral Votes by States, Presidential Elections 1932–44	126
	References	128
	Select Bibliography	133
	Index	136

Editor's Foreword

The last decade of the century is a good moment to look back at some of the dominating individuals who have shaped the modern world. *Makers of the Twentieth Century* is a series of short biographical reassessments, written by specialists but aimed at a wide general audience. We hope that they will be useful to sixth-formers and students seeking a brief introduction to a new subject; but also to the ordinary reader looking for the minimum she or he needs to know of the life and legacy of the century's key figures, in a form that can be absorbed in a single sitting. At the same time we hope that the interpretations, based on the latest research – even where there is not space to display it – will be of sufficient interest to command the attention of other specialists.

The series will eventually cover all the outstanding heroes and villains of the century. They can, as a sort of party game, be sorted into three – or perhaps four – types. Some can be classed primarily as national leaders, who either restored the failing destinies of old nations (de Gaulle, Adenauer, Kemal Atatürk) or created new ones out of the collapse of the European empires (Nkrumah, Jinnah). Others were national leaders first of all, but made a still greater impact on the international stage (Franklin Roosevelt, Willy Brandt, Jan Smuts). A further category were not heads of government at all, but achieved worldwide resonance as the embodiments of powerful ideas (Trotsky, Martin Luther

King). The great tyrants, however, (Hitler, Stalin, Mao Zedong) are not easily contained in any category but transcend them all.

The series, too, aims to leap categories, attempting to place each subject in a double focus, both in relation to the domestic politics of his or her own country and as an actor on the world stage – whether as builder or destroyer, role model or prophet. One consequence of the communications revolution in this century has been that the charismatic leaders of quite small countries (Castro, Ho Chi Minh, Gadaffi) can command a following well beyond the frontiers of their national constituency.

At the centre of each volume stands the individual: of course biography can be a distorting mirror, exaggerating the influence of human agency on vast impersonal events; yet unquestionably there are, as Shakespeare's Brutus observed, tides in the affairs of men 'which, taken at the flood, lead on to fortune'. At critical moments the course of history can be diverted, channelled or simply ridden by individuals who by luck, ruthlessness or destiny are able to impose their personality, for good or ill, upon their times. Who can doubt that Lenin and Hitler, Mao and Gorbachev – to name but four – have decisively, at least for a time, bent the history of our epoch to their will? These, with men and women from every major country in the world, are the *Makers of the Twentieth Century.*

John Campbell
London, 1990

Chronology

30 January 1882: Born at Springwood, Hyde Park to James Roosevelt and Sara Delano Roosevelt.

September 1896: Entered Groton.

1900–1904: Went to study at Harvard University.

17 March 1905: Married to Anna Eleanor Roosevelt.

Spring 1907: Passed New York bar examination.

June 1907: Became a law clerk in a Wall St. law firm.

November 1910: Elected state senator, New York State legislature.

November 1912: Re-elected as state senator.

March 1913: Appointed Assistant Secretary of the Navy.

September 1914: Defeated in New York senatorial primary.

July–September 1918: Official visit to Europe, including the battle front.

January–February 1919: Official visit to Europe.

July 1920: Chosen by Democratic Party as vice-presidential running mate to James Cox.

August 1920: Resigned as Assistant Secretary of the Navy in order to fight campaign.

November 1920: James Cox and FDR defeated in the presidential election.

August 1921: Contracted polio.

June 1924: Nominated Al Smith for Democratic presidential candidate.

April 1926: Purchased Warm Springs, Georgia.

June 1928: Nominated Al Smith for Democratic presidential candidate.

October 1928: Agreed to run for Governor of New York State.

November 1928: Elected as Governor of New York.

1 January 1929: Inaugurated as Governor.

November 1930: Re-elected to Governorship.

1 July 1932: Nominated as Democratic candidate for President.

8 November 1932: Elected President of the United States, with John Nance Garner as his Vice-President.

4 March 1933: Inaugurated as President.

March–June 1933: First Hundred Days.

June–August 1935: Second Hundred Days.

November 1936: Re-elected as President of the USA, with John Nance Garner as his Vice-President.

20 January 1937: Second Inauguration.

November 1940: Re-elected as President of the USA for an unprecedented third successive term, with Henry Wallace as his Vice-President.

August 1941: FDR and Winston Churchill met at Placentia Bay, Newfoundland and signed the Atlantic Charter.

7 December 1941: Japanese attack on Pearl Harbor.

January 1943: Attended Casablanca Conference with Churchill.

November–December 1943: Attended Teheran Conference with Churchill and Stalin.

November 1944: Re-elected President for the fourth successive term with Harry Truman as his Vice-President.

20 January 1945: Fourth Inauguration.

February 1945: Attended the Yalta Conference with Churchill and Stalin.

12 April 1945: Died at Warm Springs, Georgia.

15 April 1945: Buried at Hyde Park.

For Elizabeth and Jonathan

Map of USA in 1933

The Early Life

1

Franklin Delano Roosevelt, the 32nd President of the United States of America, was one of the most significant and influential world leaders of the 20th century. He presided over his nation from 1933 to 1945 and won an unprecedented four elections (although he was to serve only three months of his fourth term). He ranks with other great presidents such as George Washington and Abraham Lincoln, as a man who led his country in a period of deep division and crisis. During his first two terms in office, the United States suffered a major economic depression; but whilst it took the Second World War to restore full prosperity, in the intervening six years President Roosevelt succeeded in restoring America's faith in itself, retaining democracy and laying the foundation of a welfare state. He also steered his nation through the Second World War, from uneasy neutrality to full participation in the alliance which was to form the nucleus of the United Nations. Although it was during the Presidency of his successor, Harry Truman, that the fateful steps towards the Cold War and the nuclear age were taken, Roosevelt undoubtedly promoted the latter and played a part in the creation of the thorny superpower relationship which has dominated international relations ever since.

Given the sheer scale of his contribution to American history, and the very distinctive and in many cases innovative policies which he introduced, it was inevitable that President Roosevelt would become a figure of considerable historical controversy. During his lifetime, he was the subject of much adulation, yet also much bitter hatred. Historians have shown the same bewildering contradictions in trying to make sense of the man, his policies and his achievements.[1] He is regarded by some as a vital figure in the emergence of a new form of liberalism, based upon an active federal state and a socially conscious body politic. Others within the historical profession, especially those of the New Left, have adopted a more critical view of Franklin Roosevelt. They present him as a man who saved capitalism by a series of pragmatic and temporizing concessions, which simply alleviated the worst crises of the economic system. The New Deal, in their opinion, was a lost opportunity to remake the socio-economic structure of the United States.

There is, however, another interpretation of Roosevelt's contribution to American history, which sees him as neither the hero of liberalism, nor a servant of capitalism, but rather as a pragmatic politician who operated within clear and accepted constraints, and yet sought within the existing system to bring about change. He was a man who had principles, even if only of a general and rarely articulated kind, but who was far from being an ideologue. In foreign affairs, he sought to advance the best interests of the United States and to promote the cause of world peace, yet he accepted the power and domination exercised by the Soviet Union within Eastern Europe. Whatever the particular historical approach, throughout the 45 years since his death the name of Roosevelt has always conveyed a special fascination and interest – not least because, despite all that has been written about him, the man still remains an enigma, his complex personality almost impossible to penetrate.

The fascination of the man is in many ways paralleled by that of his times. He was President of the United States in an era of crises virtually unparalleled in recent history. To contend with either the severity of the world economic depression after 1929, or the onset and fighting of the Second World War, would be an immense task for any President. Roosevelt dealt with both. And whilst to a large extent the two crises were consecutive rather than simultaneous, there was a period in the late 1930s when he had to grapple with political and economic problems at home, and also growing indications of international crisis abroad. Throughout his presidency, there was no lull in the perpetual atmosphere of tension and crisis. During the last four years of his life, he acted not only as leader of his own nation, but also as one of a triumvirate conducting the entire Allied war effort, whilst additionally seeking to set the shape of the post-war world.

So Franklin Delano Roosevelt (or FDR as he is often called, to distinguish him from President Theodore Roosevelt) was a crucial figure in American and indeed world history. And yet in many ways he seems an unusual man to have achieved this, since he was born into wealth and influence, and could well have devoted his life to the traditional pursuits of an American gentleman – the profession of law and the management of his family estate. In addition, he was a cripple, having been struck with poliomyelitis at the age of 39. Moreover, although nothing was publicized at the time, he had engaged in a love affair which might well have resulted in divorce, a step which would have been disastrous for his political prospects. That he nonetheless proceeded to fill his country's highest political position, for longer than any other president either before or since, was due to his determination to succeed, his charm and self-assurance, and his shrewd understanding of the American political system. To understand the nature of the man, it is necessary to understand his background and upbringing, for they both shaped his character and moulded the confidence which marked his later political career.

Franklin Roosevelt was an only child, born on 30 January 1882 to a doting mother and a wealthy, elderly father, whose money and family connections provided the snug cocoon of a happy childhood. The Roosevelt family could date its antecedents in the United States back to the late 1640s when Klaes Martenszen Van Roosevelt left Holland for the Dutch colony of New Amsterdam. Thereafter, the family remained closely linked with New York (as it was to become), acquiring wealth through trade and real estate. In later years, the family effectively developed two main branches, one in Oyster Bay and the other on the Hudson. President Theodore Roosevelt came from the former, President Franklin Roosevelt from the latter; the two men were in fact fifth cousins, although many voters assumed that FDR's relationship to the illustrious Theodore was far closer, perhaps son or nephew. The Roosevelt family estate at Springwood, Hyde Park, where the FDR Presidential Library now stands, was one of the chain of large estates on the banks of the Hudson from which the New York aristocracy had traditionally come. Franklin was born here, the child of James Roosevelt's second marriage, to Sara Delano, who came from another Hudson family. Although Franklin had a half-brother, James (Roosevelt) Roosevelt, the latter was already in his late 20s, married and with a son of his own.

In effect, then, Franklin grew up as an only son, in an atmosphere of wealth and privilege. Hyde Park was always central to FDR's life; although he only owned it for the last three years of his life, for him it was always home. As well as Hyde Park, the Roosevelts had a summer home in Campobello island, just off the shore of

4

Maine. James Roosevelt lived the life of a gentleman from
the leisured classes, with weekly trips to New York to
deal with business and a seasonal round; spring and
autumn were spent in Hyde Park, winter in New York
City, and the summer in Campobello and in Europe. He
liked to see himself as a rural squire, a gentleman farmer,
although his money essentially came from speculation,
investment and industry. In this environment, Franklin
enjoyed a very happy and sheltered childhood. Hobbies
were well catered for, especially sailing and collecting –
stamps, stuffed and mounted birds (some shot by
himself) and, later, naval memorabilia. He made frequent
trips abroad with his parents, thus acquiring an unusually
cosmopolitan background for an American President.
Between 1884 and 1896, the family made eight visits to
Europe, spending several months at a time there. As a
result, Roosevelt acquired an excellent grounding in
French and German.

Franklin had governesses and tutors from an early age,
but due to his parents' reluctance to part with him, he
did not go to boarding school until he was fourteen.
However, his formal education was provided by the élite
establishments of late 19th-century America: Groton,
Harvard and Columbia Law School. Although Groton had
been founded only twelve years previously, it already
had an excellent reputation, and was attended by the
sons of the best American families. It preached the ideals
of public service dear to its headmaster and founder, the
Rev. Endicott Peabody, whose outlook reflected his own
schooling in England. It was from Groton that a Roosevelt
family tradition was to develop. Each Christmas, the
headmaster's father read Charles Dickens' famous work
The Christmas Carol aloud to the assembled school; this
same ritual, with Roosevelt as the reader, became a trea-
sured part of his own children's and grandchildren's
Christmases.

From Groton, FDR proceeded to Harvard. At

5

university, as at school, he rapidly conformed to the prevailing norms. He did not excel academically, averaging the 'gentleman's C'. According to most accounts, he suffered a major setback when he failed to be chosen for the most élite of the élite clubs, the Porcellian. Despite this, he was still able to engage in a wide variety of extracurricular activities, and achieved real success in his work with the undergraduate newspaper, the *Crimson*; in his fourth year, he became editor-in-chief. As such, he wrote all the editorials for a semester, but most of these were directed towards the encouragement of college spirit, the drive to win and support for the college football team, rather than wider issues. As Roosevelt ended his education, there was little sign of his having accepted any coherent pattern of thought or ideological commitment. He was still very much the product of his family upbringing and of Endicott Peabody's preaching; from them, he had acquired the attitudes, the obligations and the prejudices of a gentleman, and the beginnings of a patrician humanitarianism. From this secure background came his easy confidence and warm self-assurance.

James Roosevelt died in December 1900 whilst his son was still in Harvard. Three years later, at the age of 21, Franklin proposed to his cousin Eleanor and was accepted. This was a major blow to his mother, whose possessiveness had increased since her husband's death. Ever since, there has been considerable debate as to why Franklin chose Eleanor, since she was far from being a belle or an acknowledged beauty. Their son, another James Roosevelt, was later to suggest that FDR was looking for a woman who would not dominate him, who would be a faithful wife and a devoted mother, but who also believed in him, encouraged him, and was intelligent and thoughtful. According to a much-told tale, when FDR proposed to Eleanor, he said, 'With your help, I will amount to something.'[2] It was also true that she was more closely related than he to the current President, the Republican Theodore Roosevelt. However, it should also be pointed out that Eleanor as a young woman was attractive, graceful and the focus of much attention. Franklin married her in the face of determined opposition from Sara Roosevelt; an early sign that while he usually bowed to his mother's wishes, he would not accept her domination in major matters, as for example when he entered politics, and later insisted upon returning to the political sphere after his polio attack, despite her protests. However, in the case of his marriage, Sara merely countered his independence by extending her possessiveness and interference to his entire family.

The young couple's wedding ceremony on 17 March 1905 was graced by the bride's uncle, the first President Roosevelt, who gave her away. Thereafter Eleanor and Franklin rapidly adopted the conventional lifestyle of a fairly wealthy young married couple, in large part due to the generous, even overwhelming, gifts of the groom's mother. In May 1906 their first child, Anna Eleanor was born, to be followed over the next ten years by another five children (one of whom died in infancy). For the first few years of FDR's married life, he pursued the law profession, with three years at law school and a further three as a law clerk. However, at an early stage he decided to emulate his distant relative, Theodore, and make a career in politics. As early as 1907, he informed a fellow law clerk that he intended to become president. With his family name and Hyde Park background, once he had decided to enter politics, it was a reasonably easy ambition to realize.

It was, however, less clear which party he should represent. Franklin's father had been a Democrat, but one who had favoured limited and honest government, and disliked the populism adopted by the party in 1900. Theodore Roosevelt on the other hand was a Republican, the party favoured by most men of wealth. FDR had shown enthusiastic support for his relative's campaigns in 1900 and 1904, and had voted for him in the latter year (the first presidential election in which he had the franchise). So he could realistically have entered either party. However, in the event, the local Democratic organization approached FDR, and he thereafter threw in his lot with that party, despite its somewhat tarnished reputation in New York State. In 1910 he fought his first election campaign, for the New York State senate. A combination of vigorous and innovative electioneering (including the use of a car), his famous name and the disarray of the Republican party, all combined to win him the election. He won on personality rather than issues; although he was in favour of conservation, and willing to denounce party machines and the domination of the state by New York City, he offered little by way of concrete policies or principles.

Once he had won, FDR and his family then moved to Albany, in itself an indication of his intention to take his post seriously, since most legislators visited the state capital for only one or two days a week. However, if FDR was to secure re-election in what might well be the more normal year of 1912, he had to make his name. Again, he chose to seek publicity not through the adoption of an issue such as progressive social reform, or improved labour legislation, but through resistance to the Tammany political machine which dominated New York. In seeking to prevent Tammany from nominating their candidate, William F. Sheehan, as US Senator, FDR asserted his own independence from the party machine, whilst also attracting some national attention. Eventually another machine man, Judge James A. O'Gorman, was nominated, but Roosevelt could claim that it was his leadership of a small group of insurgents which brought about Sheehan's defeat.

In the remainder of his term, FDR did little to promote the social reform measures that were being discussed at the time, although he did vote for most of them. It was Tammany, as an urban-based machine, that had a vested interest in courting the working man. FDR, as a senator from upstate rural New York, concentrated instead on the aims of clean government, conservation and assistance to the farmers of the state – in itself a moderately progressive programme, but by no means pace-setting. Thus, in a period of progressive ferment, Roosevelt was far from a leading reform figure, playing politics rather than principles. However, his tactics proved successful, and in 1912 he secured re-election for a further two years, despite his own illness at a key point in the campaign. This victory was largely due to Louis Howe, an asthmatic journalist from Saratoga Springs, who took over Roosevelt's campaign when the latter was incapacitated. The idiosyncratic Howe, once described as a mediaeval gnome', was to remain by FDR's side until his own death in 1936, providing an invaluable source of advice, strategy and, where necessary, criticism.

The newly elected Roosevelt actually served less than three months of his second term as a state senator. This time he did not move his entire family to Albany, preferring to operate from a small rented apartment. It would appear that he had hopes of better things from the new Democratic administration under President Woodrow Wilson, whose nomination he had vociferously supported at the 1912 Democratic Convention. Those hopes were fulfilled when he was offered a number of posts, including two Assistant Secretaryships, in the Treasury and the Navy Departments. Roosevelt abandoned the New York Senate with few regrets, thus drawing to a close his legislative experience. Thereafter, his political career was to remain totally within the executive sphere. With alacrity, he accepted the post of Assistant Secretary of the Navy, which he held until 1920. This reflected his keen interest in all naval matters, but was all the more significant for FDR as it paralleled the first Washington post which Theodore Roosevelt had filled, in 1897; Franklin's plan for his own political career was modelled closely on that of the 'Rough Rider'. Like his Republican namesake, he was to prove a somewhat difficult and independent-minded deputy to the Secretary of the Navy – in this case the North Carolinian Josephus Daniels.

The major duty of the Assistant Secretary was to deal with civilian personnel, in particular the labour employed in naval yards, and hence FDR soon had experience of dealing with labour leaders. He was also involved in requests for patronage from Congressmen, although Secretary Daniels handled most other links with Congress. Roosevelt had secured Louis Howe's appointment as his assistant, and both men gave a great deal of attention to helpful political contacts, patronage especially. FDR was conscious that the most obvious next step would be for him to return to state politics and he continued to foster his support in New York. In 1914, he ran in the state primary for US Senator but, lacking the support of the party machine, he was defeated.

Most of Roosevelt's period as Assistant Secretary was dominated by the First World War, which commenced in Europe during August 1914. As a keen advocate of preparedness right from the onset of the war, FDR was far ahead of his immediate superior and, indeed, his President. He worked zealously in an attempt to build up the Navy. In his view, it was vital that the United States should have a navy at least able to undertake the tasks of national defence and the protection of her foreign trade. His sympathies were clearly with the Allies, and he chafed at the requirements of neutrality; in April 1915 he wrote to Eleanor that 'I just *know* I shall do some awful unneutral thing before I get through.'[3] When war finally came to the United States in April 1917. Roosevelt entered with enthusiasm into his wartime duties. The massive expansion in the size of the Navy which all this entailed greatly increased the scope and significance of the Assistant Secretary's responsibilities.

Roosevelt made two trips to Europe on Navy business, returning from the first in September 1918 with influenza and double pneumonia, thus putting paid to his hopes of resigning his post in order to enlist. It was at this time that Eleanor found out about his affair with her social secretary Lucy Mercer, and offered him the chance of a divorce. In a family conclave, heavily influenced by Sara Roosevelt, the couple agreed to remain together, but the affair had severe repercussions upon their relationship. Although Eleanor remained a supportive and loyal wife until Franklin's death, she increasingly developed her own interests and friendships, and began to play an active part in a number of women's organizations. One of the reasons which swayed Roosevelt's decision to remain with his wife was the recognition that a divorce would have effectively terminated his intense political ambitions. Although earlier that year Roosevelt had refused to run for governor of the state of New York, even with the support of Tammany, the decision made good political sense. Since there had been a Republican governor for the past two terms, defeat was quite possible (although in the event the Democratic candidate, Al Smith, did win). Moreover, FDR's refusal, justified on the grounds that his work as Assistant Secretary of the Navy amounted to war service, did him no harm and might even have strengthened his hand for a later election. In 1919 he made another official trip to Europe, coinciding with the peace conference at Paris, although he played no part in it. The following year, in August 1920, he resigned his post in order to run as Democratic vice-presidential candidate in the forthcoming election.

Roosevelt was an enthusiastic and able Assistant Secretary, although at times his enthusiasm ran away with him. He proved a competent administrator, but there were some differences of opinion between him and Secretary Daniels, as FDR's belligerence and enthusiasm for a 'Big Navy' clashed with his superior's pacifism and caution. Moreover, in 1920, FDR offended both the Secretary of the Navy and President Wilson, when he claimed that much of the credit for preparing the Navy for war was rightly his. This accorded with his long-held view that members of the department and the fleet waited for those periods when he was Acting Secretary to get things done. However, despite these occasional problems, his relations with Josephus Daniels were generally cordial and the older man had a considerable influence upon his junior. When FDR became President, he continued to call Daniels 'Chief', and insisted that Daniels should in turn address him as 'Franklin', a privilege shared by very few. Roosevelt held his office in the Navy Department during a particularly demanding time and played an important part in the preparation of the Navy for war.

Meanwhile, in 1920, another presidential election was due. By precedent, Wilson was expected to step down, having already served two terms. FDR therefore had to consider what direction his career should take, once the Wilson administration ended. Two obvious posts for which he might be considered were those of Governor or US Senator for New York. However, Governor Al Smith was expected to stand for re-election; and it seemed unlikely that Tammany would be prepared to support him for the latter post. With New York politics apparently closed to him, FDR's best chances of continuing in political office rested at the national level. After some shrewd lobbying on his part, the Democratic convention nominated him as vice-presidential running mate to James Cox of Ohio. Roosevelt seemed a suitable candidate in many respects; not only had he handled the convention shrewdly, but he had a well-known name, came from the East, and had been a junior member of the Wilson administration.

Once again, then, FDR's political career paralleled that of Theodore Roosevelt, who had been the Republican party's vice-presidential candidate in 1900. But there the parallel ended. Whilst Theodore had proceeded to electoral victory and eventually to the Presidency, courtesy of an assassin's bullet, Cox was defeated by the Republican candidate, Warren Harding. However, FDR ran a vigorous and nation-wide campaign, in which he focused on support for the League of Nations, a cause to which he was won in 1919, whilst returning from Europe on the same ship as Wilson. And despite his defeat, there were some positive aspects to the campaign. During it, Roosevelt acquired many of the personal staff who were to serve him during his presidency – people such as his secretary, Missy LeHand, Marvin McIntyre, who was in charge of FDR's campaign train, and Stephen Early, who acted as an advance man for the trip. Moreover, although he did not receive much national press coverage, the campaign, together with his work at the Navy Department, served to make him a well-known figure, with national as opposed to state-based contacts.

For the time being, however, FDR was out of office for the first time since 1910, and found himself relegated to the practice of law, in a decade when the Republican ascendancy appeared unshakeable. It seems fairly clear that law alone could not occupy his interests sufficiently and he became a businessman as well, engaging in a number of speculative schemes. Above all, he still hoped for a future in politics; he and Louis Howe were making plans for a campaign for the governorship of New York in 1922. But then, in the summer of 1921 disaster struck. During a summer holiday at Campobello, FDR contracted polio. For the rest of his life he was paralysed from the waist down. Although he trained himself to 'walk', using steel braces, a cane and the support of an arm, this was a difficult and increasingly painful process. The extent and impact of FDR's disability is difficult to assess, not least because he himself sought to minimize it. Indeed, it affected his political chances less than might have been expected. His privacy was respected, he was usually photographed from the waist up and the newsreels did not portray his mobility difficulties. However, it impinged upon his life on a daily basis and should never be overlooked. As Gallagher points out, in most biographies, 'FDR's disease and seven years of convalescence are treated as an episode in an early chapter in these books and never mentioned again.'[4] In assessing his future political career, not least his heavy campaigning and international travels to his wartime conferences, his immobility and dependence on others should not be forgotten.

There are those who maintain that it was in the struggle with polio that the true character of FDR was formed.[5] Whilst it undoubtedly brought him into direct contact with personal adversity for virtually the first time and may well have fed into his later humanitarian concern for the sufferings of the 'forgotten man', this is to ignore the evidence of an existing determination and careful planning for a political future. Much depends upon whether you view FDR as essentially a consummate politician, in which case his ambition and attributes were largely shaped before his illness; or as a humanitarian, a compassionate and deeply caring man, qualities which clearly would have been enhanced by his own personal suffering. It is my contention that he was in fact both.

What is clear is that FDR resisted the urgings of those, such as his mother in particular, who would have had him retreat totally from the world of politics and retire to the life of a country gentleman. He hoped for a recovery, or at least an increased use of his legs; and for the first few years after the attack, he avidly pursued any conceivable chance of a cure. Finally in 1924 he discovered the waters at Warm Springs, Georgia, which he bought in 1926 and which became a second home. In the meantime, however, his name was not allowed to slip from the public or the party consciousness. This was largely the responsibility of surrogates and especially his wife.

Schooled by the loyal Louis Howe, Eleanor began to play an increasing role in the Democratic party organization and even branched into speechmaking. She played an active part in the State Committee's Women's Division and worked hard on behalf of Al Smith's national campaigns. Louis Howe also remained with Roosevelt, surrendering plans for a lucrative business position in order to organize and plan FDR's political future.

Meanwhile, even if FDR could not run for office himself, he could retain his links with those who did. Thus, in 1922 he pressed Al Smith to run again for the governorship of New York, and in 1924, nominated him as a Democratic Presidential candidate, in a speech in which he referred to the New Yorker as the 'Happy Warrior' – a phrase which might well have been applied to himself. The party ultimately chose John W. Davis as their candidate; however, Roosevelt had gained by running Smith's campaign. He had built up nation-wide contacts with Democratic leaders. Moreover, as a rural, patrician, Protestant politician, it did him no harm with the many Democratic voters in the cities to be seen to be backing Al Smith. FDR nominated him again in 1928. This time, Smith was the final choice of the Democratic Party, but not of the American electorate. In the United States of the 1920s, an Irish Catholic urbanite like Smith stood little chance of becoming president. Roosevelt meanwhile had been slowly building a power base for himself within the national party.

In that same year, Roosevelt's own political career was reactivated, when he agreed to run for Governor of New York, yet another post which Theodore Roosevelt had held en route to the White House. This was the obvious next step for FDR to take, but he was genuinely reluctant to embark upon the campaign. He had just made a major financial investment in Warm Springs; furthermore, the improvement which he had shown since discovering the springs had encouraged his hopes that he might eventually walk again. Politically, moreover, the signs were that 1928 would be a Republican year, given the widespread prosperity. Defeat was thus possible and a third electoral defeat in a row might well destroy his chances of a political comeback. Nonetheless, after remaining incommunicado for as long as possible, FDR finally capitulated to the strong pleas from Al Smith. For Smith, it was critical to his presidential ambitions that he should carry New York and thus the strength or weakness of the man running as Democratic contender for the governorship would be crucial. FDR had the upstate rural background which most prominent Democrats in New York lacked and might well swing the state, not just for himself but also for Smith.

Once having yielded to Smith's pleas, FDR swung into the fight with vigour, and fought a lively and active campaign. Having no allegiance to Tammany, he could hope to appeal to Republicans and independents as well as the party loyalists. He did so, however, by promising to build upon Al Smith's progressive record, rather than offering a new programme of his own. Although he only won by a margin of 25,000 votes out of a total of 4.5 million votes cast, he nonetheless succeeded in his campaign, unlike Al Smith, who failed not only to win the Presidency but also to carry his own home state of New York. In the course of the campaign, in a period from 17 October to the beginning of November, FDR travelled 1,300 miles and made nearly 50 speeches. This clearly did much to answer fears that he was physically incapable of holding down the job of governor. It now remained to see whether during his incumbency, he could succeed, not only in dampening fears relating to his polio, but also in making so positive an impression that he might realistically look to the presidency in the future.

The Governor of New York

2

On 1 January 1929 Franklin D. Roosevelt took the oath of office as Governor of New York upon his Dutch family bible – the same bible used for all his subsequent inaugurations. Thus began a virtually continuous period of executive office which was to last until his death.[1] Two months later the successful Republican candidate, Herbert Hoover, was inaugurated as 31st President of the United States. Both men's careers were to be transformed by the scope of the economic depression ushered in by the Wall Street crash later on that same year. By a cruel irony, Hoover, born in poverty and the symbol of charitable endeavour through his work as Food Administrator in the aftermath of World War One, had his career totally blighted by his apparent failure to respond to the suffering caused by the Depression; whilst FDR, the son of wealthy and privileged parents, with no direct experience of large-scale charitable work, made New York a model of how to turn the resources of government to the task of relief. However, one must beware of viewing Roosevelt's gubernatorial term as though it were entirely dominated by the Depression. The stock-market crash did not come until near the end of his first year in office and it was some time before it became apparent that this was not a temporary setback but a full-blown depression. It is important to examine Roosevelt's governorship as reflecting his own political philosophy and concerns, rather than as simply the consequence of Depression-dictated responses to crisis.

A picture emerges from such an examination of a man who is best described as a cautious progressive, with reforming instincts, but by no means a radical reformer. Many reform initiatives were strongly influenced by others, such as Frances Perkins (his Labour Commissioner) and his wife Eleanor. Roosevelt was well aware of the political realities with which he worked and during his four years as governor demonstrated a considerable ability to work within those constraints to the best possible purpose. Perhaps the two most significant constraints were public opinion and the complexion of the state legislature. That the two were not necessarily the same is demonstrated by the fact that while Roosevelt was twice elected as a Democratic governor, in both terms he had to contend with a Republican-dominated legislature, which saw no political gain in allowing him to appear dynamic and successful. He had also to safeguard his own political future, in the short term represented by the need to win re-election in 1930. As he could be fairly sure of carrying the Democrat-dominated city, he had to direct much of his effort to the rural upstate regions which were traditionally Republican. Their interests were, fortunately, close to Roosevelt's own; he was genuinely keen on agriculture, conservation and the general well-being of the farmer. These state-oriented priorities had to be pursued as well as his national ambitions, which were increasingly centred upon the Presidency.

In 1929, however, FDR's first task was not so much one of policy as of power. He had made a resounding political recovery after his apparent elimination by disability, but he had now to prove that he was capable of being a positive and active governor. Ultimately, the main opponent against which his efforts were directed was the state legislature, but the first challenge came from his immediate predecessor, Al Smith, who had served a total of eight years as governor. Although the New York electorate had failed to support Smith in the 1928 presidential election, he still hoped to exercise power from behind the scenes. The new governor was urged to retain Smith's entire cabinet, or, failing that, at least the services of Robert Moses as Secretary of State and Belle Moskowitz as speechwriter and adviser. However, Smith had badly underestimated the man whom he had pressed to succeed him. If Roosevelt was to be more than simply a Smith shadow, he had to make a firm stand, not least because both men were possible contenders for a future Democratic presidential nomination. Since he intended to continue many of Smith's progressive policies and initiatives, FDR had to assert his independence by rejecting the Smith entourage and patronage. Sixteen of the existing eighteen department heads were left in post, but the two most significant figures of the Smith years, Moses and Moskowitz, were soon eased out of their key roles. FDR also went against Smith's opinion when he appointed Frances Perkins as Labour Commissioner. This independent stance earned him the enmity of his predecessor, but eliminated any possibility that Roosevelt might be seen as no more than a Smith protégé.

Having broken free of Smith, Roosevelt had next to assert himself against the Republican legislature. This was to be a continual and critical battle over the next four years. However, in an early foretaste of his tactical political skill, FDR was nonetheless able to achieve a great deal. In his first year as governor, he challenged the legislature over control of the budget, a campaign which ultimately succeeded, although only after a prolonged and bitter battle. He played upon the Republicans' close identification with the rural interests in the state by making agricultural matters a key part of his first session. He was also able to force through a proposal to establish a commission on old-age security, an issue on which he felt personally sympathetic. However, the legislature blocked many of his more progressive initiatives, on judicial reform, hospital construction and labour, only to find that this rebounded against them, as many of these were popular with the voters. The following year, 1930, the Republicans sought to prepare for the elections by passing several reform measures, albeit in a watered down form; this enabled FDR to claim that he had successfully converted them. He was proving an adept and skilful executive, more than a match for the hostile legislature.

Right from the beginning of his governorship, Roosevelt was developing the unique style of administration and leadership that continued into the Presidency. The Executive Mansion in Albany became not just a busy family home, but the centre of a hive of activity, incorporating advisers, officials, personal staff and his family, who played an increasingly important part in his political activities. Eleanor was of particular significance, for despite spending three days a week in New York, where she taught in a school she jointly owned, she still continued large-scale entertaining and the maintenance of her own political interests. Roosevelt had already formed the habit of drawing much of his political inspiration from a tight schedule of discussions and informal meetings with an eclectic group of people. He impressed many with his quick grasp of new issues and his tremendous memory. Meanwhile, he established his own personal popularity, demonstrating what was to be one of his major political skills – the ability to relate to the ordinary voter, in speeches, tours through the state and homely radio addresses. His keen interest in all matters pertaining to the state and his ability to manipulate the existing system to his own needs emerged at a very early stage in his executive career.

Governor Roosevelt was more than simply a shrewd political tactician, however. His reputation as a reform governor was based upon initiatives taken even before the Depression struck. Thus, he pressed for prison reform, improving the physical conditions within the prisons themselves and seeking to change the parole system. Frances Perkins was encouraged to press ahead with a number of innovatory labour and social measures, such as a compulsory reduction in working hours for women, child labour controls and a proper workmen's compensation system, and also to tackle other safety and health issues. Roosevelt himself supported an investigation into the provision of state security for the needy old and the possibility of an insurance contributory system for wage earners. In June 1930, at the annual Governors' Conference, he became the first state governor to call for unemployment insurance and old age pensions. Although in part a response to the immediate crisis, this initiative also reflected ideals which he had been developing from the beginning of his governorship; in particular, he recognized the interdependence of all sectors of society in a mature industrial economy like the United States.

However, the main issue upon which Roosevelt focused in his first term as governor was conservation and the development of water power. In his years at Albany, he took a particularly keen interest in the operation of electricity utility companies and the investigation of their profit margins. This was by no means a new issue, as Al Smith had first raised it, but Roosevelt pursued it eagerly. The cost of electricity in New York state was considerably higher than the rates prevailing just the other side of the border in Canada, a fact which Roosevelt graphically illustrated by pointing to the comparative costs of running basic household appliances like stoves and irons. Although the electricity industry was run by private companies, the governor maintained that the state should play some regulatory role, for example to ensure fair pricing levels. Roosevelt also proposed the exploitation of the enormous hydro-electric potential of the great St Lawrence river. This commitment to the regulation of private utility companies, together with a belief that if necessary the public sector should operate some utilities to set yardstick rates and practices, had not only state-wide but also national implications. FDR was able to use the issue with great success to tap into progressive reform sentiment throughout the country as a whole.

Moreover, the question of the rates charged for electricity was of great importance to the upstate farmers and rural middle classes – all traditional Republican voters. Traditionally Tammany bosses of the Democratic state machinery had concentrated upon the city, leaving the rural areas neglected, resentful and Republican. This situation was exacerbated by the general dissatisfaction among American farmers in the 1920s, as the agricultural sector suffered a steady decline. FDR, as an upstate New Yorker himself, hoped to rectify this situation. In 1929 he went on a tour of the rural areas, an excursion which he was to repeat each year. This had the additional purpose of proving that the strain of office was not too much for the governor. Although FDR could not himself inspect the interiors of the numerous state institutions at which he stopped, Eleanor acted as his surrogate, a role she continued later as First Lady. At his instigation, she learnt to ask penetrating questions and report back to him later in great detail. In all, FDR did much to please the agricultural sectors of New York state, as was shown when he carried the upstate regions in the 1930 election.

By giving so much attention to the farmers, FDR was actually following his own instincts, but at the same time he was pursuing his battle with the Republican-controlled

legislature. The Republicans could not afford to antagonize their rural power base. It was thus impossible for
them to oppose many of Roosevelt's measures which
were aimed at the farmer, such as a reduction in farm
taxes, the funding of rural roads through a gasoline tax
and improvements in rural education. Meanwhile their
failure to pass several substantial measures of benefit to
the urban industrial classes, groups which were traditionally Democratic anyway, could be blamed on the legislature rather than the governor. Additionally, the governor
could use for his own benefit the party split between
executive and legislature; on measures on which FDR was
comparatively half-hearted or downright conservative
(such as a reform of the banking laws) he could allow
the Republican legislature to be blamed for inaction. In
his continual battle with the legislature, FDR rapidly
assumed the posture of being the governor of all the
people, above the rough-housing of everyday politics and
party advantage. This has close parallels with his later
practice as President.

It is important to consider the pre-Depression
measures at such length, not only because they
demonstrate the developing political skills of Roosevelt,
but also because they underline the fact that his policies
were not just Depression-dominated responses to crisis.
The governor was not simply creating a safety net in New
York; he also had an appreciation of long-term structural
problems in need of solution. The reforms which he had
been implementing before the Depression show clearly
that he appreciated the dangers of following a completely
laissez-faire policy in an industrialized state – as illus-
trated by his support of Frances Perkins' innovations. In
many cases he was not so much initiating policies
himself, as responding to the requests of others. Again,
there are parallels with his later period as President,
where he provided the environment which enabled
reforms to be implemented, without necessarily himself

dictating the shape those reforms would take. In FDR's first term as governor, therefore, he dealt with a wide range of political, social and economic problems. His popularity as governor was reflected in a landslide victory in the 1930 elections, which he won by a massive 750,000 votes. But even before his re-election – overwhelmingly after it – he had to contend with the devastating impact of economic depression.

The 1920s had been a period of unparalleled prosperity within the United States, but the move towards a mass-consumption economy was insufficient to counter several major structural weaknesses within the American economy. The agricultural sector had been weak since the early 1920s, as a glut of primary commodities on the world market caused prices to collapse. The banking sector was fragmented and lacked effective central control, so that it was easily affected by over-extended credit policies. Both of these problems were significant within the specific New York context. And the international economy had also been dislocated by the First World War. The Wall Street crash of October 1929, together with the international banking crisis of 1931, caused these latent flaws to emerge into the open. In itself, a stock-market crisis need not affect a country's overall economic performance, but in 1929 it was associated with other economic problems. During the next four years, the economic indices continued to move firmly downwards.

Nonetheless, many believed that this depression could be tackled, as all previous depressions had been, by a combination of market forces and exhortation. This was the approach taken by President Hoover and, initially, Governor Roosevelt. But even if the economy would right itself in time, the extent of human suffering demanded attention. By the autumn of 1932 approximately 13 million people were out of work. The bank crisis which hit in the years 1931–3 wiped out the savings of literally millions of Americans. Many were destitute; and those in need soon found that the lack of state welfare benefits cast them upon the poor law or private charity, both of which were to be stretched to the utmost by the sheer scale of the disaster. In the large industrial cities, where the unemployment rate was highest and where all classes were being hit by economic disaster, charity was quite simply inadequate. It was this phenomenon of mass suffering, typified for many by the images of breadlines and apple-sellers on the streets of New York, that Governor Roosevelt had to address. But the problem was not confined to the urban centres. Agricultural distress had existed even during the prosperous 1920s and was greatly exacerbated by the Depression. FDR had also to consider the problems of the upstate rural areas, from which he drew so much of his support and identity.

Given the nation-wide scale of the cataclysm, one might expect that President Hoover, well-known as a humanitarian, would immediately turn his attention to the problems of the destitute and starving. However, this was not to be the case; yet Roosevelt, by his response to economic disaster, was able to enhance his national standing. To some extent, the different responses of the two men reflected the federal system of government prevailing in the United States. The two main levels of government, federal and state, were assumed to have different, if complementary, functions. The federal government, it was generally agreed, had only the most limited role *vis-à-vis* social policy, such as welfare, social security and labour matters. Hoover's own predisposition to rugged individualism was thus supported by the conventional view of the role of federal government. Although often castigated by commentators for his failure to anticipate the New Deal, Hoover did in fact seek to encourage private enterprise to respond positively and imaginatively to the economic crisis, and in the creation of the Reconstruction Finance Corporation demonstrated his recognition of the importance of pump-priming. But he relied predominantly on market forces to secure recovery. FDR, on the other hand, needed no scruples about turning his attention to the task of relief, a duty that state governments had clearly within their purview.

Initially, however, Governor Roosevelt, like the vast majority of Americans, simply failed to recognize the scale of the problem and assumed that relief for those in need should be handled at the local, not the state or federal level. He paid very little attention to economic issues in the 1930 election, which was largely fought upon issues of corruption and electric power. Nonetheless, as he came to recognize the sheer scale of the problem, he initiated an innovatory and successful programme. During 1931 he set up a Commission on the Stabilization of Employment and also called for investigations into the provision of unemployment insurance. Recognizing that individual states might be reluctant to impose the cost of state welfare benefits on business lest they move elsewhere, in January 1931 he called an interstate conference of the governors of the main industrial states, to see whether it would be feasible for them all to pass social welfare legislation simultaneously. As it became apparent that local and private relief could not meet the scale of the suffering, Roosevelt decided that the state must take responsibility. Although this went contrary to many of his political beliefs, he held that 'Our Government is not the master but the creation of the people. The duty of the State towards the citizens is the duty of the servant to its master.'[2]

Thus, in the summer of 1931 he presented to a special session of the legislature proposals for a Temporary Emergency Relief Administration (TERA), to be financed by additional taxation, which would provide state-funded relief for the needy. At this stage, he still hoped to meet the extra expenditure from current income rather than borrowing. The legislature voted a total of $20 million, to be split equally between public works and work relief. A young social worker, Harry Hopkins, was employed as administrative director and soon demonstrated the enthusiasm and commitment that he later brought to the national stage. By February 1932 over 150,000 New Yorkers were on work or home relief; however, by then TERA had virtually exhausted its funds, while the numbers actually unemployed exceeded one and a half million. In order to ensure its continued existence, Roosevelt accepted the need to borrow money by a bond issue. New York was the first state to take such positive responsibility for the unemployed. Roosevelt was also the first major political figure in the USA to advocate unemployment insurance. But whilst Roosevelt was in some respects anticipating the New Deal, he had not yet developed a full programme. Thus, he did very little to regulate the state's banks, even though a quarter of the nation's bank accounts were in the state of New York and even though he was probably aware that the Bank of the United States was in trouble (it crashed in December 1930). Nor did he use any of his powers as governor to regulate the New York Stock Exchange. However, he rapidly emerged as one of the most active and responsive political leaders in the United States. He was also developing his ideas on the interdependence of society and the duties of the State which were to underpin the later New Deal.

By his progressive and innovative policies in New York, Roosevelt had established his claim to be considered for national office, a claim that was further enhanced by his sweeping re-election in 1930. His political ambitions definitely included the presidency and both he and Louis Howe had been planning towards that end, at least as early as the vice-presidential campaign of 1920. However much he protested in public that he had no thoughts of the presidency, in his second term he was working not only at state politics, but also at expanding his support within the Democratic party, with his eyes firmly fixed upon the 1932 election. In so doing he was to portray himself as a progressive and sought to link the Democratic party with progressive causes, thus challenging the conservative elements which were so strong within the Democratic National Committee. Moreover, progressivism was traditionally popular in the West, where FDR hoped to acquire a great deal of support. Despite his somewhat lukewarm support for social reform in his first years in politics, therefore, Roosevelt was emerging as one of the key liberals within the United States. However, while he had a strong claim to the Democratic nomination, so too did a number of other candidates, amongst them the defeated 1928 candidate, Al Smith; and with the Democrats now in a strong position to reverse the long-standing Republican domination of the Presidency, competition was fierce.

If he were to secure the presidency, FDR had to win two separate, if interlinked campaigns, the first for his party's nomination and the second for the presidency itself. As regards the former, FDR had many advantages; he came from one of the major centres of Democratic politics and had served his party for a long time. As Governor of New York, he had been overwhelmingly re-elected and had offered a humanitarian and compassionate programme to deal with the tribulations of economic crisis. However, he faced a strong challenge from Al Smith, who had also established a sound reputation as a progressive governor, and who could count upon a lot of support from the urban wing of the party. The chairman of the Democratic National Committee, John Raskob, was behind Smith. Thus, Roosevelt's nomination was far from a foregone conclusion. In order to win, he would have to be better organized and better known than the other hopefuls. Fairly soon after the election victory in 1930, Louis Howe set up a formal 'Friends of Roosevelt' office, drawing upon a national network of contacts which they had maintained and expanded in the years since 1920. Meanwhile, Roosevelt was building up a strong team to support him, including his counsel, Sam Rosenman, who had been writing speeches for him since the 1928 campaign and Raymond Moley, a political scientist from Columbia University. These two men were later to be joined by a group of academics and experts, including Adolf Berle and Rexford Tugwell, to form what became known as the 'brain trust' – a group which provided information, ideas, contacts and speeches for Roosevelt on a wide variety of themes. Many of them were specialists in economic matters, of which Roosevelt knew very little, but which were clearly going to be central in the election. This helped FDR combine the administration of the state of New York with a punishing schedule of speeches, on a whole variety of topics, including many national issues, which he had hitherto avoided as incompatible with the tasks of state governor. In terms of political strategy, he could turn to Louis Howe and also to his Secretary of State for New York, the Bronx boss Ed Flynn, who had supported him even before his victory in 1928. An important addition to the Roosevelt camp was Jim Farley, the affable secretary and later chairman of the state Democratic Committee. Farley was a superb political manager and had a network of national contacts.

With a carefully structured organization behind him, Roosevelt was thus well placed to launch his official campaign for the presidency in the Democratic party primaries, beginning in January 1932. His main goal was to convince doubters that he had a firm hold on the issues that mattered, whilst not alienating key groups of his supporters. To do this, he often had to temporize, or straddle important issues, such as that of the League of Nations. Despite his long-held belief in the efficacy of the League, in February 1932 he declared that the United States should not join that organization as then constituted. It is thus hardly surprising that the prominent commentator Walter Lippman wrote on 8 January 1932 that FDR was 'an amiable man with many philanthropic impulses, but he is not the dangerous enemy of anything. He is too eager to please'.[3] Even so, there were hints of a more radical orientation, as in his radio address on 7 April 1932, in which he referred to 'the forgotten man at the bottom of the economic pyramid'.[4] On 22 May 1932 he delivered a powerful address at Oglethorpe University, Georgia, in which he called for an end to waste, referred to the existence of 'poverty among abundance' and seemed to imply the need for some kind of national economic planning to make the system 'fair'. It was in this speech that Roosevelt called for 'bold, persistent experimentation', and argued that 'It is common sense to take a method and try it. If it fails, admit it frankly and try another. But above all, try something.'[5] This admirably encapsulates the methodology of the later New Deal.

However, despite all his efforts, when the Democratic convention met at the end of June 1932, Roosevelt was still about 100 votes short of the two thirds majority of delegates required by the party convention rules. It was only as a result of frantic activity by Farley and Howe, and a complex deal whereby FDR accepted as his vice-presidential running mate the conservative Southerner, John Nance Garner, that Roosevelt was finally nominated on the fourth ballot. In a dramatic gesture, he flew to Chicago to accept his party's nomination in person. This highly uncomfortable night flight was a complete break with precedent, which dictated that the candidate-elect should remain as though in purdah until formally notified by his party of his nomination, a process which could take some weeks. It indicated therefore that despite his physical disability, Roosevelt intended to wage a determined and energetic campaign. On his arrival at the convention, FDR made a speech that was to become famous, not so much because of what it said, but because of one key phrase within it. In talking to his party, Roosevelt asserted, 'I pledge you, I pledge myself, to a new deal for the American people.'[6] That phrase, the 'New Deal' was used in a cartoon the following day, and soon became synonymous with his policies and later presidential programme.

So, by July, having already set the brain trust in place, with a Democratic platform acceptable to him, and a new Democratic party chairman (Farley) in place of Raskob, FDR was now set to fight the second campaign, that for the presidency. If anything, this was easier than the first; the Republican party had renominated Hoover, who was irremediably linked with the economic disaster that had engulfed the United States. Nonetheless, campaigning in the months leading up to November was intense. Opponents of Roosevelt had two possible weapons which they could use against him. One was to emphasize his lack of experience in areas such as monetary and economic policy and international affairs, arguing that it was vital to retain the continuity and expertise represented by Hoover. On the whole, however, Roosevelt was able to avoid those issues on which he was weak. The other was to question his physical fitness to assume the presidency. During the 1930 election, he had sought to defuse fears about his health by having himself examined by a panel of insurance company doctors, following which 22 companies agreed to insure him for very large sums at normal rates. In 1932, all in the Roosevelt camp were at pains to minimize his disability. When asked how she felt about her husband's physical capacity to withstand the strains of the presidency, his wife responded, 'If polio did not kill him, the Presidency won't.'[7] Probably the best answer to such concerns was the vigorous campaign waged by Roosevelt, in which he travelled about 13,000 miles, making 16 important speeches and a further 67 less significant ones.

Inevitably, however, the main focus of the presidential

campaign was likely to be the issues, in particular economic issues. The Democratic platform pledged the party to a repeal of the 18th Amendment which had established prohibition, but otherwise, apart from a declaration of support for unemployment and old age insurance at the state (as opposed to federal) level, and an advocacy of banking and investment reforms, it gave little indication of policy. Roosevelt himself relied predominantly upon generalizations, especially in the field of economic policy; and while calling for bold action failed to specify what form that bold action would take. Given the difficulties faced by Hoover in trying to win support for his discredited policies, FDR could afford to play a cautious game. In so doing, at times he appeared to out-Hoover Hoover, pledging himself to rigid economies in federal government spending and a balanced budget. Roosevelt basically concentrated upon telling people what they wanted to hear; speeches were tailored to the needs of a highly specific audience. Inevitably, then, there was some degree of contradiction and blurring of the issues. Yet some of his speeches were more radical – such as the well-known speech of 23 September at the Commonwealth Club in San Francisco, written for him by his most radical brain trusters, Rexford Tugwell and Adolf Berle. In this he yet again attacked the consequences of economic concentration, criticized the actions of 'financial Titans' and businessmen, and suggested that the government had a duty to act in order to redress the decline in equality of opportunity and to develop an economic declaration of rights for the American people. While bewildering at one level, this lack of a coherent, detailed programme could be seen as an excellent illustration of pragmatism and experimentation in action.

This inevitably leads to the vexed question of whether – and to what extent – FDR foreshadowed in his election campaign the programme of the New Deal. That he intended his campaign to be more than simply an exercise in political pragmatism is demonstrated by his assembly of the brain trust. Since many of his advisers advocated new and even, on occasion, radical views, these were often reflected in Roosevelt's speeches, as in the Commonwealth Club speech. As against that, both Moley and Tugwell could cite examples – in the areas of tariff and agricultural policy – where they had been asked by the candidate to somehow combine into one speech two totally contradictory policies. The mixture of ideology and pragmatism means that while it is possible to point to a number of specific references in particular speeches which appear to presage later elements in the New Deal, such as for example the speech on agricultural policy on 14 September at Topeka, Kansas, one cannot argue that FDR actually outlined a coherent programme of measures which might be identified by the name. On the other hand, nor should it be assumed that he was no more than a voice-piece for his more academic speech-writers. FDR worked with them and modified drafts considerably; it is hard to imagine him actually giving utterance to sentiments with which he was not, at the very least, sympathetic. Roosevelt was a shrewd politician, who in his own uncertainty mirrored that of the American people. In seeking electoral victory, he was prepared to compromise in an effort to maximize support. This reflects the lack of any clear theoretical base to Roosevelt's political agenda, but also the fact that throughout the campaign he was only gradually crystallizing his views, aided by the intense tutoring of the brain trust.

In the event, on polling day (8 November) FDR won by a landslide – 22,809,638 votes to 15,758,901. In the electoral college, he carried 42 states, as against Hoover's six. But although FDR knew in November that he was to be the next President of the United States, it would not be until early March that he actually assumed the reins of office. This would give him time to assemble a staff and a cabinet. In the meantime however, Hoover, as the outgoing president, would find himself without any real authority to take decisive action. The problems of the interregnum at times of crisis had been graphically illus-trated in 1860, at the time of the Civil War. Now Hoover found his hands tied for a critical four months, during which time the financial crisis deepened, both domesti-cally and internationally. The global financial situation was precarious, as country after country quit the gold standard and economic nationalism prevailed. Clearly, an international initiative was required to meet the problem; equally clearly, Hoover was ill placed to take it. During the interregnum, he made several efforts to persuade Roosevelt to join with him in seeking a way out of the Depression. While this was in itself a praiseworthy goal, however, Hoover did not invite co-operation or consult-ation; in effect, he asked Roosevelt not only to endorse Hoover's own policies as the only feasible ones, but also to commit himself to following those policies in the future. Roosevelt refused, therefore, to act in accord with Hoover and the relationship between the two men deve-loped into one of mutual dislike.

FDR's behaviour during the interregnum did not appear that of a man weighted down by the responsi-bilities of office. Although behind the scenes he was making appointments, receiving reports and generally preparing the nucleus of at least a part of his legislative programme, his outward demeanour was that of a man without a care, as he went on vacation and generally relaxed. For a man about to assume an arduous task, this was no bad strategy, but it did not suggest a preoccupa-tion with the problems which would face him when he assumed the presidency. The interregnum did offer one dramatic incident, however, when in February 1933 an attempt was made upon Roosevelt's life in Miami. Although the President-elect was unhurt, Anton Cermak, the mayor of Chicago, was fatally wounded. All who were present were impressed by Roosevelt's calm demeanour – not least because he was totally unable to move himself out of danger. Reports of the event made a powerful impression upon the public, but few Americans realized at the time how momentous it would have been had the assassin hit his target.

The First New Deal, 1933–35

3

Although Franklin Roosevelt was of global significance as a wartime leader, the New Deal was his most important contribution to the USA. The New Deal was both a product of the American past, reflecting the American ideological, economic, political and social framework before 1933; and also a precursor of later reform programmes which implemented many of the goals which it had originally set. Many historians have distinguished two New Deals, the first centred around a policy of co-operation and accommodation with business, the second more concerned with social welfare and tending towards an anti-business direction.[1] Although this ignores certain continuities throughout the New Deal years, there was undoubtedly a shift in emphasis, clearly discernible in FDR's speeches and policies, and hence this discussion of his domestic policy will employ the 'two New Deals' framework.

The nature of the New Deal agencies, the beliefs and objectives of the people who ran them, and the overall effect of the myriad programmes, is beyond the scope of this brief biography. Instead, it will concentrate upon the contribution of the man who directed the initiatives, determined priorities and provided the inspiration and rhetoric which underpinned the hard administrative endeavour – Franklin D. Roosevelt, who was inaugurated as the 32nd President of the United States on 4 March 1933, in a ceremony traditional in its trappings, but surrounded by the threat of economic and social collapse. As he took the presidential oath on the steps of the Capitol, his hand rested upon his family bible, open at the thirteenth chapter of St Paul's epistle to the Corinthians – 'And now abideth faith, hope, charity, these three; but the greatest of these is charity.' A host of problems faced the new President, of which the most immediate was the US banking sector, which lay in ruins. In many states the governors had closed the banks by decree rather than see them close their doors against their depositors. Meanwhile, the number out of work was estimated to be as high as 17 million people (around 25 per cent of the workforce); whilst even those in employment had experienced cuts in hours and wages. With no nation-wide system of old age pensions, unemployment insurance, or relief, many Americans suffered the steady erosion of living standards, and even total destitution and starvation. Roosevelt faced a demoralized and shattered nation.

The new President immediately demonstrated one of his primary political skills; the ability to mobilize and express the popular will. His first inaugural address, delivered in the chill of a March day in Washington D.C., presented little that was concrete, with policies, such as they were, expressed in generalities. It did however contain two important messages for the American people. The first was that the main problem they faced was one of morale rather than just specific concrete difficulties. 'First of all, let me assert my firm belief that the only thing we have to fear is fear itself – nameless, unreasoning, unjustified terror.' The other was that here was a president prepared to act. This was an emergency, roundly declared the President, and the only thing to do in a real emergency was to take the necessary powers to deal with the problems. Comparing the crisis to a state of war, Roosevelt made plain that if the normal constitutional and legal processes failed to respond to the immediate difficulties, then he would look for extraordinary powers to compensate. 'This Nation asks for action, and action now.'[2]

Even as the customary celebrations accompanying any inauguration continued, FDR emphasized the mood of emergency and swift action. The new cabinet was rapidly sworn in, and met the day after the inauguration (a Sunday). What would be the new administration's priorities? FDR had, after all, taken an equivocal line during the election campaign. Nor was it immediately apparent from his cabinet what shape the New Deal would take for, in common with all American cabinets, it was an attempt to pay political debts, win support and defuse potential threats. The most innovatory appointment was that of Frances Perkins as Secretary of Labour, thus making her the first woman ever to be appointed to a US cabinet post. Roosevelt's cabinet included both liberals and conservatives, close associates of the President and those with whom he had very little acquaintance, Democratic party stalwarts and independent Republicans. It was however notable that the conservatives tended to be concentrated in the economic and financial posts, such as William Woodin as Secretary of the Treasury; whilst liberals dominated in the social and spending departments, such as Labour and the Department of the Interior (headed by Harold Ickes). This was a reflection of Roosevelt's own inclinations, but it suggested that the evolution of a united cabinet policy would be far from easy. In such a situation, the President's own power and direction was considerably enhanced, as he was responsible for reconciling two possibly incompatible camps. Places were also found in the administration, although not in the cabinet, for the chief figures of the brain trust, for example Raymond Moley and Rexford ·Tugwell. Roosevelt's tendency to rely heavily upon informal advisers, rather than upon his cabinet members, served to concentrate power in his own hands even more.

The new administration rapidly sprang into action, although many cabinet members had as yet no programme to meet the immense problems they faced. A national three-day bank holiday was proclaimed; meanwhile, Congress was summoned into special emergency session on 9 March. In this first Congressional session of Roosevelt's term, a session which lasted exactly one hundred days, a number of highly significant measures were passed, addressing not only the economic but also the major social problems faced by the nation. Most of the bills were sent to Congress by the president and, in all, fifteen pieces of legislation were passed into law at breakneck speed, covering a wide range of topics, from agricultural policy to conservation, from industrial policy to relief, from banking to the end of Prohibition. The staccato pace of the 'First Hundred Days' was unprecedented. Impelled by the sense of utter urgency and crisis within the country as a whole, both houses of Congress allowed themselves to be swept along in the torrent of legislation which poured from the White House. The question that must be posed is whether this first manifestation of Roosevelt's policies represented a coherent programme, or was simply a piecemeal response to pressing problems. To do this, it is necessary to examine the legislation a little more closely.

The first point to make is that Roosevelt did not have a structured and complete programme with which to present Congress. He had originally intended only to push through a few key pieces of emergency legislation; however, finding that Congress appeared remarkably amenable and that the public mood was in favour of prompt and drastic action, the president simply kept

going. This accounts for the random order in which the
various bills were sent to the Hill, with the main industrial
recovery measure coming very late in the day. As
Congress assembled, FDR's immediate priority, under-
standably, was banking, but the Emergency Banking Bill
was in fact a measure designed to assist the recovery of
the existing banking system, and had been drafted by
members of both the outgoing and incoming adminis-
trations. With a national bank holiday already in existence, the Treasury reopened only those banks which it
deemed to be 'sound'. By mid April about 70 per cent of
the nation's banks were open. The second thought was
to cut government spending, a move which many would
see as regressive and one which was in total opposition
to all that the later New Deal stood for. Then the next
step was to bring about the end of Prohibition. In other
words, the early stages of the Hundred Days were
initially conservative, and aimed at meeting the election
platform commitments of the Democratic party.

However, later measures were more radical. FDR had
initiated discussions on agricultural policy even before
his inauguration, and rapidly introduced a measure, the
Agricultural Adjustment Act (AAA), which worked on the
presumption that if production levels were kept down,
prices would rise. To prevent individual farmers from
increasing their own production in order to compensate
for declining prices, they were paid for reducing their
productive acreage, using funds raised by a tax on food
processing. On industrial policy, the signs were that
Roosevelt had not yet reached any firm conclusions.
However, when Congress began to discuss their own
proposals, including inflation and the compulsory reduction of hours to thirty per week, the president had to act
quickly, and did so by rapidly canvassing opinion and
seeking to incorporate as many proposals as possible
into the final bill, the National Industrial Recovery Act
(NIRA). In addition to a massive appropriation ($3.3

billion) for public works, it also provided for self-regulation and co-operation among businessmen. In order to avoid cut-throat competition and increase demand, the codes set up to regulate each industry had to include the provision of maximum hours and minimum wages; in return, some elements of price-fixing and production control were allowed. This structure had strong parallels with the industrial planning of the First World War and, as then, also included provisions for some rights of collective bargaining. Both the AAA and the NIRA worked on the principle of encouraging scarcity in order to push up prices, and both included income-boosting measures, which might ultimately increase consumption – the payments to farmers in return for reducing production and, in the case of the NIRA, minimum wages provisions. To facilitate price rises, the US dollar was taken off the gold standard in April. The acceptance of big business and large-scale commercial agriculture, and hence the reduction of competition, was implied in these major economic recovery initiatives, as was the need for centralized national planning of the economy.

None of the measures described above could be described as socialistic or as threatening the existing status quo. Rather more radical, and close to Roosevelt's own interest in conservation, was the Tennessee Valley Act, one of the few reform measures in a session otherwise dominated by recovery and relief. The Tennessee Valley Authority (TVA) created under the act was a model of how conservation, planning and the provision of employment and rural assistance could be achieved. It was a multi-state public enterprise which generated hydroelectric power, built model housing and dams, improved navigation, engaged in flood control and soil conservation and manufactured cheap fertilizer. This massive experiment in public ownership was totally unprecedented, although the genesis of some of the ideas underlying it can be seen in FDR's own concern with public power and navigation in New York. Through the efforts of the TVA, and the later creation of the Rural Electrification Administration, rural life was transformed by the widespread introduction of electricity.

There still remained the problem of the millions of needy Americans. To help those in work who were threatened with the loss of their homes, a Home Owners' Loan Corporation was set up, which refinanced mortgages. Small bank deposits were guaranteed through a Federal Deposit Insurance Corporation. But what of the millions who were unemployed? In his first inaugural speech, Roosevelt had declared that 'Our greatest primary task is to put people to work,' and this, he hoped, would ultimately be achieved by industrial recovery and public works programmes. However, this could not solve the most immediate problem of caring for the unemployed. So in a major departure from tradition, federal funds were provided for the relief of those who were unemployed and destitute. By declaring that the national government had an obligation to work for the well-being of the individual citizen, albeit only in times of dire emergency and on a temporary basis, Roosevelt was going far beyond what other presidents had contemplated. FDR's own contribution to the question of relief was the suggestion of a Civilian Conservation Corps (CCC), a band of young men paid to carry out conservation work across the country. Although imaginative and immensely popular, it could cater for only a small number of those in need. To meet the problems faced by the vast majority of the unemployed and needy, the Federal Emergency Relief Administration (FERA) was created under the leadership of Harry Hopkins. In order to surmount constitutional difficulties, the states were involved in both the financing and the administration, with some adverse consequences. Even so, large sums of federal money were granted to the states, and by August 1933 over 18 million people were being assisted by FERA funds.

Thus, in the first four months of his presidency, Roosevelt had inaugurated policies aimed at assisting business, farmers, labour, the unemployed and the needy. The First Hundred Days offered something to almost everyone and tried to set up a compromise of interests, in which the gains of, say, business would be offset by the protection of consumers and workers. This attempt to set up a broker state, trying to keep all the groups in society within a coalition, distinguished the first stage of the New Deal, and reflected Roosevelt's own beliefs and ideas. The frantic introduction to the New Deal was seen by many contemporaries as an exciting innovation, a clear sign of a federal government prepared to act decisively in the face of crisis. Yet what – if anything – distinguished the philosophy of the New Deal at this stage? It does not appear to have been motivated by any clear-cut ideological commitment. As Raymond Moley commented of the New Deal as a whole, 'to look upon these policies as the result of a unified plan was to believe that the accumulation of stuffed snakes, baseball pictures, school flags, old tennis shoes, carpenter's tools, geometry books and chemistry sets in a boy's bedroom could have been put there by an interior decorator'.[3] It certainly brought about no major structural changes in the socio-economic fabric of the country, but was rather a response to events and to the massive scale of human suffering and economic collapse. No long-term social reform of any substance was mooted; but then, maybe, this was neither the time nor the place. The New Deal's primary attribute was its eclectic nature and its willingness to bow to the tide. In that respect, it reflected the personality of the man who presided over it.

It should be stressed that this does not mean that Roosevelt alone drafted or initiated the bills presented to Congress. Indeed, some measures dated from the Hoover presidency, and were simply expanded, publicized and implemented by FDR – for example, large-scale public works, the banking legislation of 1933 and the Reconstruction Finance Corporation, used as a major source of federally provided credit. Many other important measures owed their genesis to individuals or groups other than Roosevelt himself. Thus, Roosevelt's response to the problem of unemployment was the CCC; but it was at the instigation of others that FERA, public works and a programme for industrial stimulation were drawn up. The AAA and the NIRA bills were largely drafted by advisers and other influential individuals working in co-operation, and Roosevelt took little detailed part in them.

However, as in his New York years, it was Roosevelt who remained in overall control. No cabinet member or adviser, however influential, was delegated with the supervision of the entire programme; it was impossible to point to any one individual as being Roosevelt's right-hand man, or *de facto* prime minister. Few of his cabinet members or brain trusters had the political experience or ability to work with Congress or party. This pattern of working was very much the Roosevelt style. He sought suggestions and advice from a wide cross-section of opinion and frequently requested several separate individuals or agencies to work on the same piece of legislation. This meant that the only underlying philosophy could come from the President himself and he showed little sign of having a complex or sophisticated philosophy to offer. FDR frequently horrified his advisers by suggesting that they should solve the dispute between two completely different and even contradictory proposals by welding the two together. The result was often confusion. The President was more of an enabler, providing the kind of atmosphere in which others, more expert than himself, could come together to put forward proposals. And yet FDR was the one who decided what measures should be put forward and when. This system served to concentrate the final decision and directions in Roosevelt's own hands; however, it also created an imaginative and innovative set of measures. The lack of philosophical underpinning which many commentators have seen in the New Deal, was a reflection of the president's own hazy ideas. FDR had a strong patrician humanitarianism and a dislike of personal suffering, and this was clearly reflected in the New Deal. However, his economic objectives were less clear-cut. In truth, FDR was far more of a politician than a reformer.

Whatever the limitations of the first manifestation of Roosevelt's programme, the sheer scale and rapidity of the administration's response, so in keeping with the message of the first inaugural speech, did much to restore public confidence. So too did the demeanour of the President and his undoubted ability to communicate with the American public. A good example of this came at the time of the Emergency Banking Act which was, as already explained, a fairly conservative measure. The banks were to be reopened – reorganized, to some extent reformed, but intrinsically little changed from before. Had this gesture failed, then it would have cast severe doubts upon the rest of the New Deal. But Roosevelt turned the tide in favour of both the Banking Act and his own programme. To do so, he used the medium best suited to his own magnetic charm. The radio was still in its infancy but sufficiently widespread to enable him to reach out to the American people. It has been estimated that his first presidential broadcast was heard by some 60 million people. On 12 March, only two days after the Banking Act had been passed into law, FDR addressed his audience in terms which suggested that he was conducting a private conversation with each individual, seated by his own hearth – the so-called 'fireside chat', the first of many. Beginning with the words, 'I want to talk for a few minutes with the people of the United States about banking,' Roosevelt did little more than assure them that the reorganized banks were now safe – 'I can assure you that it is safer to keep your money in a reopened bank than under the mattress.'[4] But where the American public had doubted the bankers, they believed him. The following day, when many had expected a rush to take out money as the banks reopened, deposits actually exceeded withdrawals. FDR might not have a coherent platform to offer, but he had the pulse rate of the American people.

This close and immensely personal communication with the ordinary man and woman in the street was a critical part of the entire Roosevelt presidency. It was assisted by his excellent working relationship with the White House press contingent. He normally held two press conferences each week, ensuring that the public were kept informed of the president's movements, activities and views. In turn, the American public kept Roosevelt in touch with their opinions. Vast numbers of letters came to the White House, expressing the writers' views, their fears, their requests for assistance and often their thanks. These letters were carefully monitored and in many cases acted upon, however small the favour asked. To handle the avalanche of mail reaching Roosevelt and his wife daily, the mailroom staff had to be increased from one to fifty. Americans felt that they knew their president personally, as they heard his warm voice and informal words through the airways, and as his characteristic pose – head thrown back, with tilted cigarette holder in mouth and old-fashioned pince-nez spectacles – was captured again and again on film.

It was often remarked that Roosevelt settled into the presidency as though he had been born to it. Certainly, it represented a goal for which he had been striving for a great many years; he was no stranger to the White House, from both the days of Theodore Roosevelt and his own experience in the Wilson administration. Although for the President Hyde Park would always be home, the White House became his family's main residence for twelve years, from March 1933 until FDR's death.

Life there rapidly took on the informal Roosevelt impri-
matur, stressing that this was not just an official residence, but also a family home. It was an extended family
which lived there; although the Roosevelt children were
largely grown up, with spouses and homes of their own,
they and their own children were frequent visitors and
occasional residents. So too was Roosevelt's mother, who
died only three years before her son. Rooms were found
for close Roosevelt intimates – Louis Howe, Missy
LeHand and later Harry Hopkins. In 1937 James Roosevelt became part of his father's official entourage, as one
of his secretaries, but this was less than successful. Work
and leisure blended together, not only for the Roosevelt
clan, but also his office staff, who regularly enjoyed pre-
dinner drinks mixed by the President, and took part in
lively social events such as the Cufflinks Club meetings
held each year on the President's birthday (on one occasion, Roosevelt dressed as a Roman emperor and female
guests as vestal virgins).

Some changes had to be made to the White House in
recognition of Roosevelt's disability, including the
construction of a swimming pool with funds raised by
public subscription. Both as the President and as a
cripple, it was impossible for FDR to mingle unnoticed in
normal social gatherings. However, he did all that he
could to keep in touch with a wide cross-section of
opinion, in part by bringing people to him. The White
House was the centre of much hospitality, both formal
and informal, although the food was notoriously poor (a
reflection of Eleanor's disdain for matters of the table).
Individual conferences with advisers, experts and anyone
else likely to be of use were regularly held, both at lunch
time, when the president was often joined at his desk for
a snack meal, or even in morning conferences at his
bedside, where he had breakfast and scanned the
morning's papers. His charming and cheerful manner
soon put visitors at ease, as did the ebullient atmosphere

which surrounded him. Frequent trips to Warm Springs and Hyde Park continued, together with fishing trips and sea voyages. Yet obviously, there were limitations upon the freedom of movement of any president for security reasons; in the case of Roosevelt, these difficulties were compounded by his handicap, although permanent ramps were constructed at the entrances of the buildings he used most frequently, including St John's Church in Lafayette Square.

It is difficult to assess how far the public was conscious of the extent of FDR's paralysis. He was at great pains to create the illusion that he was far from a helpless cripple, using his braces to help him 'walk' short distances on key occasions. Although he had a small, light wheelchair, built around an adapted kitchen chair, he never used this in public. In an era before daily television news broadcasts, most shots of the president were still photographs and the press seem generally to have respected his wish that no shots of him should be taken that displayed his helpless legs. However, he made no attempt to hide the fact that he had had polio and brought it to public prominence once a year, when gala balls were held on his birthday, to raise funds for the treatment of crippled children. By 1937 there were some 7,000 of these balls, attended by more than three million Americans. He also helped found the National Foundation for Infantile Paralysis, which funded the treatment of, and research into polio. The balls, and other appeals headed by the President, raised $1.8 million in 1938, while in 1945 the total was a staggering $18.9 million. These funds, and the work of the Foundation, did much to pioneer the successful treatment of polio.

Although surrounded by people, and rarely alone, FDR had very few really close intimates or lifelong friends. His closest supporters were Louis Howe, who died in 1936, his secretary Missy LeHand, who had been his constant companion since 1920 and, last but not least, his wife.

However, ever since the Lucy Mercer affair, the Roosevelt marriage had been more of a working partnership than a romantic relationship. This trend was to continue and increase during the presidential years. Eleanor Roosevelt had been far from happy about Roosevelt's elevation to the Presidency, fearing that it would seriously affect her own freedom and activities, such as her teaching, lecturing and work with a number of women's groups. However, although some of those activities were necessarily curtailed, others flourished. She became even more the 'eyes of the president', carrying out visits and reporting back to him on all she saw. Her lecturing and writing continued; indeed, she began a daily syndicated column, entitled 'My Day'. In effect, Eleanor Roosevelt created the modern role of the 'First Lady' and turned it into an important position in its own right. Nor did she hesitate to use her influence with the President on behalf of causes and groups dear to her, although not always with success. As her independent role grew, she was more often away from the White House. Nonetheless, like so many of those with whom FDR came into contact, she found herself serving his purposes as he pursued his political and reformist objectives.

FDR was the hub of the White House; he was also the dominant centre of his administration, in the sense at least of overall direction. He certainly cannot be described as a great administrator. He lacked the interest in organizations and method which was necessary to create a smooth-running and efficient bureaucratic machine. His refusal to delegate completely, his penchant for retaining ultimate personal control, his propensity for competitive administration, despite the internal feuding that it produced, can all be seen as faults, signs of a man anxious to retain total control and direction. Yet in other ways, FDR's determination to maintain personal control had beneficial results. Particularly after December 1934, when he made plain that all legislative proposals originating in agencies and departments should first be approved by him, the legislation presented by the executive to Congress represented a centralized programme; the tradition that the president should have a legislative programme was firmly established by him. He avoided alternative power bases being created within his cabinet and was able to utilize to the full his ability to spot and captivate human talent. As no one was able to establish a power base other than through the wishes of the President, he was able to manipulate the prima donnas within his administration. On the other hand, once the main framework of a policy or agency was in place, FDR was capable of allowing considerable scope for innovation to the hundreds of administrators who thronged to Washington D.C. and who relished and thrived upon the heady atmosphere of action and change.

Thus, in the period after the First Hundred Days, FDR was content, having set up the framework of the New Deal in a short exhaustive burst of legislation, to leave its implementation to those who were involved in the host of 'alphabetical agencies' – the NRA, the CCC, the TVA, the AAA, the FERA, the PWA and others. The AAA began to enforce production cuts, while the National Recovery Administration (NRA), under the direction of General Hugh Johnson, set up industrial codes by a combination of evangelical fervour and the 'Blue Eagle' campaign (companies which had signed up with the NRA were allowed to display a blue eagle, as a visible symbol of their commitment). There were some new measures – for example, the Securities Exchange Act of 1934, which imposed considerable restraints upon stock markets. Additional steps were taken to assist the farmers. And, in an effort to push up prices, Roosevelt adopted a number of inflationary schemes which manipulated the gold content of the dollar. But on the whole, the president held his hand, hopeful that the major economic recovery measures would be effective and that the economy would soon begin to show definite signs of improvement. Meanwhile, having committed himself to a domestic programme, FDR continued to distance the United States from any international initiatives intended to bring about a co-operative approach to the economic depression, such as the London Economic Conference held in June 1933.

For many ordinary Americans their first direct contact with the New Deal came in the form of relief. Under FERA, federal money began pouring into the states, bringing relief to millions of Americans. In an attempt to minimize need and suffering over the winter months and avoid a psychologically damaging repeat of the previous winter, the federally funded Civil Works Administration (CWA) was set up in November 1933, providing work programmes for the unemployed and those on the relief rolls. Some of the work projects consisted of 'made work', such as leaf-raking and were ridiculed as 'boondoggling' in the press, but others were of real value to the community, including the construction, repair or improvement of roads, the building of playgrounds, repair of public buildings and similar schemes. Some four million Americans participated in the CWA during the few months of its existence. As the various relief programmes began to operate, an ever-increasing number of Americans were assisted by the federal government. Relief incomes were far below average wages, but were a welcome alternative to the stark realities of destitution, or even minimal relief doles from local or state sources. Never before had the federal government so directly touched the lives of its citizens, bringing them in many cases from the edge of despair. As one American later commented, 'I can remember the first week of the CWA cheques ... Instead of walking around feeling dreary and looking sorrowful, everybody was joyous ... If Roosevelt had run for President the next day, he'd have gone in by a hundred per cent.'[5] Many attributed this aid directly to Roosevelt, who had shown that he and his administration, at least, remembered the 'forgotten man'. In a fireside chat in June 1934 he rhetorically posed the question, 'Are you better off than you were last year?'[6] For the vast majority of Americans, the answer was 'yes'. Unemployment fell, albeit only slowly, a relief safety-net was created, and by the end of 1934 the national income was up by $9 billion, an increase of nearly 25 per cent over the previous year.

However, as the economy began, very slowly, to improve during the rest of 1933 and into 1934, and as the sense of crisis passed, disappointment grew with the limitations intrinsic to the various schemes. The farmers wanted more than payments to restrict production voluntarily; they wanted to be free to set their own levels of production, yet be guaranteed fixed prices which met their costs. The businessmen resented the increasing regulation, the need to give concessions to labour and the possibility of ever higher taxes to pay for the relief programmes. Labour, meanwhile, was discovering that a determined employer could find ways round the NIRA labour provisions without too much difficulty. And consumers found that the prices of the goods they bought were increasing. This dissatisfaction increased after spring 1934, as the slow signs of recovery in the economy ended and stagnation set in. Tension grew as it became apparent that prosperity was not just around the next corner. The New Deal, it was now clear, would achieve no miracles, no instant economic recovery. Although in the mid-term elections of November 1934 the Democratic party won an incredible victory, actually increasing their majority in Congress, there were growing criticisms of Roosevelt's policies. A number of groups were showing their discontent, with increased labour conflict and the threat of radicalism within the farming community. Radical state politicians gained national prominence with their progressive platforms – men such as Governor Floyd Olson of Minnesota, the La Follette brothers in Wisconsin and Mayor Fiorello La Guardia in New York City. The numbers of unemployed were still far too high; those helped by federal relief were considerably less than the total number in need.

Thus, many Americans began to look beyond the New Deal, in particular to a number of charismatic dema-gogues, who offered attractive, if often simplistic, pana-ceas to cope with economic crisis. Although financially impractical, schemes such as Dr Francis Townsend's revolving pensions (by which those over 60 would be paid $200 a month, on the condition that they spent the entire sum within the period) and Huey Long's Share-our-Wealth programme (including massive redistribution of wealth and a national minimum income) were immensely popular, particularly amongst the poor and the old. Father Charles Coughlin, an advocate of silver-based inflation, won over many Americans through his mastery of FDR's own medium, the radio. All of this suggested that a growing number of people were no longer satisfied with FDR's leadership. Roosevelt was par-ticularly concerned by the threat posed by the 'Kingfish' – Huey Long, Democratic senator for Louisiana and the man whom he once described as one of the two most dangerous men in the United States.[7] The latter's political ambitions were considerable and probably focused upon 1936, the year when Roosevelt would be seeking re-elec-tion. If Long ran as an independent, he might just attract sufficient votes from Roosevelt to allow in a Republican. At the same time, criticism of the New Deal was growing from the right, as the growth of federal regulation of busi-ness and the failure of NIRA to bring about complete recovery alienated many businessmen. They began to demand a return to balanced budgets, limited govern-ment and the abandonment of social reform. By the summer and autumn of 1934, FDR faced increasing oppo-sition from both sides, a slackening-off of the never par-ticularly spectacular economic recovery and, of course, the urging towards more reform, as opposed to recovery measures, from advisers such as Perkins and Tugwell. In effect, he had to decide which was the most threatening source of opposition and move to counter it.

In the event, he decided that he could best afford to antagonize the right (traditionally allied to the Republican party). At the very beginning of 1935, therefore, there were signs that he was beginning to move to the left. In his State of the Union message in January 1935, the president called for social reform, with the emphasis on social security and employment, stressing that 'the ambition of the individual to obtain for him and his a proper security, a reasonable leisure and a decent living throughout life, is an ambition to be preferred to the appetite for great wealth and great power'.[8] The Social Security bill was already being drafted by a special cabinet committee. This would address the serious lack of welfare provision within the United States, by setting up nation-wide systems of social insurance and encouraging a more uniform level of security programmes. A programme of old-age insurance coupled with old-age assistance was proposed, to counter the fact that aid was provided for the needy aged population in only ten states.

In the same month, a new relief programme was proposed, the Works Progress Administration (WPA), which was based upon work relief (rather than direct relief, or the dole) for the employables. Although for many WPA workers, the jobs provided were heavy manual labour (or, in the case of women, sewing projects), a number of highly imaginative schemes were devised, particularly for professional groups. Research programmes were implemented, while artists, musicians, actors and writers were provided with schemes which directly related to their skills. Ultimately, over eight million workers were assisted by the WPA before its demise in 1943. FDR was perhaps trying to ensure that he retained the support of those without work, who were humiliated by the receipt of a 'dole'. But in addition, it would fit well with the Social Security bill, the idea being that long-term needy requiring direct relief – the old, the disabled, the blind, etc. – would be catered for under its provisions, while the WPA provided immediate short-term and emergency assistance for those in dire need. By May a massive Emergency Relief Appropriation Act, providing nearly $5 billion, enabled the WPA to make serious inroads into the provision of works projects and also provided funds for the Public Works Administration (PWA) and rural reform, in the shape of the Resettlement Administration.

However, even if Roosevelt was already looking for a way of galvanizing the reform spirit, progress was slow. The Social Security bill soon faced obstacles and objections in Congress, and it took five months to secure the required emergency appropriation. Nor did the President appear to be taking any initiative to address the stalemate, until, in May 1935, came another setback which made firm action imperative. The Supreme Court, which had already declared some New Deal measures unconstitutional, now posed a real threat to its fundamental structure. In a famous ruling *Schechter Poultry Corporation v. United States*, the Court declared unanimously that the key provisions of the National Industrial Recovery Act were null and void, as they exceeded the powers granted to the federal government under the Constitution. In so doing, they ignored the undoubted fact that in a national economy, powers of regulation could not be left solely to the individual states and made plain that they were opposed to any extensive federal government intervention in the economy. President Roosevelt was furious, declaring that as a result of the court decision, 'we have been relegated to the "horse-and-buggy" definition of interstate commerce'.[9] There was now a considerable risk that the Supreme Court would also find against other

New Deal laws, especially as many of the emergency acts had been hastily drafted. If the Court proceeded to dismantle more of the New Deal, it would leave FDR looking weak and incapable. In 1936 the Supreme Court also invalidated crucial elements of the AAA, the Guffey Bituminous Coal Conservation Act and the New York State minimum wage law. However, even before this, Roosevelt had acted decisively to recapture the political initiative. In so doing, he launched what is often referred to as the Second New Deal, which will be examined in the next chapter.

The Second New Deal, 1935-38 4

The 'Second Hundred Days' in the summer of 1935, although less concentrated than the First Hundred Days, represented Roosevelt's successful bid to regain the political initiative following the Supreme Court's body blow. At the same time, it underlined the growing emphasis within the administration on reform rather than merely relief and attempted recovery. Many of the most permanent achievements of Roosevelt's New Deal date from those summer months. The decision to launch another period of intense legislation was apparently taken at short notice. In June 1935 Congress was preparing to adjourn for the summer, when FDR sent a message to Capitol Hill, demanding the enactment of five 'must' bills and threatening to keep Congress in session throughout the hot steamy Washington summer unless the bills were passed. The measures concerned were the Social Security bill; the Wagner Labour bill; the Public Utilities Holding Company bill; a banking bill; and a new tax measure. By late August Congress had indeed passed all five measures, albeit with some modifications, together with a sizeable number of minor bills. For contemporaries and in the view of many historians the Second Hundred

Days initiated a second New Deal, different in substance and objectives from the first. In fact, the change in emphasis was more gradual and limited in scope than is often implied. However, the New Deal had taken a leftwards step, and by so doing had not only signalled Roosevelt's defiance and determination to the Supreme Court, but had also undermined the popularity of the Townsend Revolving Pensions and Share Our Wealth Schemes.

This is not to say that the sudden burst of energy which heralded the 'Second Hundred Days' was simply the response to threats from the demagogues and the Supreme Court. Some of the measures, notably the Social Security bill and, to a lesser extent, the Holding Companies bill had been in the process of formation over a very long period and represented months of careful planning. Indeed, before she accepted the post of Secretary of Labour, Frances Perkins had demanded a commitment from FDR that he would incorporate long-term social reform into his programme. As for the privately sponsored National Labour Relations (Wagner) bill, FDR had decided to throw his support behind it three days before the Schechter decision. However, by his ultimatum to Congress and by the new 'soak the rich' tax message, Roosevelt demonstrated the political purpose of the Second Hundred Days. The 'must' legislation was far from coherent when taken as a whole, either in its ideology or its origins. Nonetheless, rather than being an emergency programme, it represented an attempt to address seriously some of the long-term problems in the American socio-economic structure and put them to rights. The most short-term measure – the attempt to raise taxes – was the least serious of all the five bills and was considerably diluted by Congress without too many regrets on the part of FDR.

What, then, were the consequences of the legislation passed by Congress in this intense session? Organized labour was given a number of guarantees to reinforce collective bargaining, including a clear definition of just what constituted 'unfair labour practices' on the part of employers. A complex social security system was set up, providing old age and unemployment insurance, which was to be funded by payroll taxes, together with a federal–state funded system of grants to certain categories of 'unemployables', including the needy old, the disabled and mothers with dependent children. Action was taken against the giant conglomerates in the public utilities, especially the power industry, to control them in the interest of the public. Under the banking act, control over the money supply was radically altered, with power being shifted to the federal government away from the private banks. The Federal Reserve was given greatly enhanced powers over credit and the supply of money. The tax measure, as ultimately passed, introduced graduated inheritance and gift taxes, together with a tax on excess corporate profits. All of these considerably extended the power of the federal government on a permanent basis, and created for the national government a social responsibility which had hitherto been reserved primarily for the states.

By now, FDR had clearly abandoned any thoughts of a co-operative, centrally planned political economy, opting instead for a campaign against big business, in the form of redistributive taxes, legislation against holding companies and the expansion of government control over banking. This marked a shift in emphasis away from the first New Deal of 1933, which had accepted and worked with big business. It is this which has led many commentators to talk of a Second New Deal. The difference between the two has been summed up thus: 'The First New Deal characteristically told business what it must do. The Second New Deal characteristically told business what it must *not* do.'[1] Accompanying this switch in emphasis was a change in Roosevelt's main advisers, as Moley and Tugwell (both keen advocates of central-ized economic planning) were effectively replaced in Roosevelt's counsels by others, such as Ben Cohen and Tom Corcoran, who were anxious to see the restoration of competition. The anti-business orientation of the administration should not be over-emphasized, for the New Deal was still doing more to preserve American capi-talism than to undermine it. However, the president had begun to make plain that in a democracy, the national government had to serve the interests of all the people, not just a privileged minority. FDR was now distin-guishing a clear 'enemy' – those wealthy men whom, he claimed, fought the democratic decisions of the New Deal and sought to undo its achievements. By January 1936, he was beginning to speak of 'the small minority of busi-ness men and financiers, against whom you and I will continue to wage war'.[2]

It is important to bear in mind the limitations, as well as the achievements, of the Second Hundred Days. First of all, although there were some acts incorporating a few of the features of the NIRA, such as the Connally 'hot oil' Act and the Guffey–Snyder Act (which regulated the coal mining industry) there was no national programme for industry as a whole. The attempt to impose central planning upon the economy, never more than half-hearted at best, was now clearly over. Secondly, although there were some social justice measures, they certainly did not go very far and did nothing to alter the funda-mental structure of society. There was no provision for medical services, many of the most needy groups were excluded from the social security legislation (such as domestic and agricultural workers), and the federal government made no contribution to the old age and unemployment insurance funds. The cumbersome state–federal system set up in the social security provisions has been rightly described as a 'crazy-quilt'.[3] Nor was there any substantial redistribution of wealth, despite the so-called 'soak the rich' tax measure. Not only was the original proposal comparatively limited in scope, but Congress further modified it, replacing a graduated corporate income tax with a tax on excess corporate profits. Moreover, after this short burst of legislation, the president showed no inclination to carry on with reform in 1936.

With the passage of the major measures of the Second Hundred Days, the main legislative structure of the New Deal was virtually complete. Additional bills were passed by Congress over the next three years, including in 1936 the Soil Conservation and Domestic Allotment Act to replace the AAA, and the Fair Labour Standards Act (FLSA). However, they were limited in number, and for the most part built upon the ideas and programmes already in place. The numerous agencies continued to effect the daily life of millions of Americans; aid was extended to the farmers affected by the horrendous dust storms in the Mid-West; the PWA and the WPA built roads, schools, hospitals, houses, and even warships and planes. However, at the federal level, there were few new initiatives for reasons which will be examined below. What, then, can we say about the main achievements and limitations of the New Deal?

The New Deal was not a complete innovation in American politics. Many of its ideas and methods had parallels in two of the other leading reform programmes of the twentieth century, Theodore Roosevelt's New Nationalism and Woodrow Wilson's New Freedom. But influential though these two presidents had been in Roosevelt's political education, the New Deal was more than just a continuation of the age of reform. In its reorientation of the role and power of the federal government it had re-written the agenda of American federal politics. The federal government had involved itself in the direction of the economy to an extent never before envisaged; it had actively intervened to assist organized labour and give relief to the needy; and it had set up the framework of a social security state. The banking and securities systems had been reorganized, reformed and supervised. It had also effectively countered the threat from radicals and demagogues, particularly with the death of Huey Long in September 1935 at the hand of an assassin. There were, however, many groups which had not benefited from the New Deal to the extent that their desperate plight demanded – sharecroppers, tenant farmers and the blacks among others. In short, compared with what had gone before, the New Deal was a radical departure, but Roosevelt and the members of his administration were trying to improve the existing American system, not replace it. They had reformed the worst abuses of the capitalist order, through the provision of social security, old age insurance, minimum wages, industrial welfare and the encouragement of organized labour, but they posed no threat to the private enterprise system.

In the process of establishing and consolidating a New Deal, FDR had also created a new Democratic party, albeit one with strong legacies of the past. The solid conservative Southern wing, so typically represented by Vice President Garner, was still very strong within the Democratic party; it was not until 1940 that FDR felt sufficiently confident to unseat his rebellious running mate in favour of another northern liberal. As we will see below, the party machine continued to defy him. But in terms of the voters, the 1936 election saw the clear emergence of a new Democratic coalition, forged out of the underprivileged groups which FDR had helped during the preceding four years. Thereafter, the Democratic party dominated in the urban sectors of the United States, and hence in Congress. It was not purely a product of the previous term; in many ways, it represented the fruition of trends which had been building up over a number of years. But it was under FDR that the new Democratic coalition emerged, with a solid core of blacks, organized labour, ethnic minorities and the underprivileged at its heart. In an amazing reversal, even the traditionally Republican black Americans began to support the Democratic party, which had been for so long the symbol of white supremacy. In a concrete manifestation of this change of support, many blacks replaced the pictures of Abraham Lincoln on their walls with ones of Franklin Roosevelt, whilst in the 1936 election some 75 per cent of northern blacks voted for FDR. The Democratic party dominated in the urban Northern cities, allowing it increasingly to become the party of liberal reform. And the symbol of this changed image was President Roosevelt himself. Roosevelt, the man who had never had to rely purely upon his salary, who had always enjoyed the lifestyle of the landed gentry, was seen as the man of the people and represented the Democratic commitment to urban liberalism and underprivileged groups.

As FDR was building up his reputation among the poor, his standing amongst the wealthier classes of society sank ever lower. On the face of it, this is difficult to understand. Roosevelt was, after all, in many ways one of them. He enjoyed, even during his presidency, yachting trips hosted by the Astors and other wealthy friends. Nor were the rich as badly affected by the New Deal as they maintained. The Second World War was to prove far more egalitarian, in terms of government-directed redistribution of wealth. Indeed, a strong argument can be advanced for Roosevelt as the saviour of capitalism – and hence, presumably, of capitalists. Yet it is still necessary to take heed of the almost hysterical hatred demonstrated by many wealthy individuals, hatred so extreme that they often refused to call him President Roosevelt, but instead referred to him as 'That Man in the White House'. Years afterward, one businessman said of FDR that 'He was the great destroyer.'[4] This irrational behaviour, together with more concrete examples of conservative opposition in the form of the Supreme Court and the Liberty League, contributed to FDR's shift from a political rhetoric based on a universal appeal – the true broker state – towards a much more class-oriented approach, which is most clearly revealed in the 1936 election campaign against the Republican candidate, Governor Alfred Landon of Kansas. And yet the bitter hostility of his words was not matched by deeds. Even during the election year of 1936, FDR did little to justify the hatred with which he was regarded.

The central class-based theme of his campaign began in his acceptance speech in June 1936, in which he castigated the 'economic royalists', whose shuttered vision of the United States would rule out all reform or federal assistance to the unemployed and destitute. Perhaps he saw what so few did; that if his class was to survive, as a privileged élite within American society, it had to recognize the suffering and aspirations of the majority of the population. Undoubtedly, the rich themselves contributed to the bitter rhetoric by their own unrestrained attacks upon Roosevelt. He, however, responded in kind. 'Never before in our history have these forces been so united against one candidate as they stand today. They are unanimous in their hate for me – and I welcome their hatred. We know now that Government by organized money is just as dangerous as Government by organized mob ... I should like to have it said of my first Administration that in it the forces of selfishness and of lust for power met their match. I should like to have it said of my second Administration that in it these forces met their master.'[5] The division of the American public on class lines was underlined by the fact that for the first time, the unions formed a nationwide political association, the Labour Non-Partisan League, which threw its support behind Roosevelt.

The other main theme in the campaign was to emphasize the improvement in the state of the nation during the four years since the last presidential election. Economic recovery still lay a long way off, but all the economic indices registered a considerable improvement. This was a fact recognized not only by the poor, who voted for Roosevelt in large numbers, but also by many progressive businessmen and even Landon himself, who as Governor of Kansas had endorsed many New Deal measures. The success of FDR's attempts to create a new progressive coalition was demonstrated by the scale of his victory. He triumphantly carried the Northern cities as well as the solid South and the West, trouncing his opponent in a devastating landslide victory. In the popular vote, he won by 27,476,673 votes to Landon's 16,679,583 votes. He carried every state except Maine and Vermont, thus giving him a majority in the electoral college of 523 votes to eight. In a campaign which had been intensely personal, and in which the key issue had been Roosevelt's New Deal versus the 'economic royalists', FDR had won an overwhelming mandate.

As he began his second term in January 1937,[6] all the indications were that he would use that decisive electoral mandate to institute more radical reforms. The assumption that social reform would be the hallmark of his second term is borne out by his second inaugural speech, delivered on 20 January 1937, in which he spoke poignantly of 'one-third of a nation, ill-housed, ill-clad, ill-nourished'. He further emphasized this theme of improving the lot of the underprivileged when he added, 'The test of our progress is not whether we add more to the abundance of those who have much; it is whether we provide enough for those who have too little.'[7] He had a massive Democratic majority of 245 in the House of Representatives, whilst the party provided 76 of the 92 Senators. The path seemed clear for a third 'Hundred Days', even more reformist than the other two. However, as we examine the record of Roosevelt's second term, what is striking is not the wealth of reform legislation, but its paucity. There are some achievements, undoubtedly, including a major agricultural act, the FLSA and other administrative successes, such as the continuation of large-scale relief and public works. The significance of this last point should not be underestimated, especially as regards the millions of Americans still dependent upon state and federal assistance of some kind. But compared with the phenomenal record of the first term, and the hopes raised by the rhetoric of 1936, then the years up to 1940 are ones of disappointment. By the end of 1938 the New Deal had effectively run out of steam; a formidable conservative opposition had developed, in the country as well as in Congress; and, even more devastating, no real economic recovery had taken place – indeed, in 1937 the United States experienced a deep recession. In explaining this reversal of fortunes, there are a number of factors which have to be taken into consideration. Some were of course beyond the President's control, as witness in particular the course of foreign affairs, which absorbed more and more of his time. However, it must be concluded that some at least of the blame rests with FDR, partly because of a lack of clear goals and also partly as a result of serious tactical errors which this normally very shrewd political operator made, especially in the realm of the struggle with the Supreme Court.

FDR had been considering possible strategies for reforming the Supreme Court ever since that august institution had first acted against New Deal legislation. In February 1937 he presented to Congress a plan to achieve the restructuring of the federal judiciary. Thus, despite a second inaugural speech suggesting a major programme of social reform, FDR chose instead to devote his first legislative session to the reform of the Supreme Court. The necessity of addressing the court issue at a fairly early stage in the second term cannot be denied. The Social Security Act and the Wagner Act were likely to come before the Court before long, and its decisions on other labour law indicated that the Wagner Act in particular might have a rough passage. However, the president gave the Court no chance to reconsider its position in the light of his popular mandate. That is not to say that the Court, an appointed not an elected body, would necessarily have been swayed by popular opinion. But given the splits among the justices, between liberals, conservatives and waverers, the 1936 results might have prompted some second thoughts. Indeed, later events were to suggest that a judicious delay might have been beneficial.

In addition, Roosevelt's normally sure political touch had deserted him, for he made a number of critical errors. He sprang the plan upon Cabinet and Congress with no prior consultation, and without first ensuring that the large Democratic majorities within the legislature would remain loyal to him on this matter. It soon became apparent that this loyalty could not be counted on and that it would be extremely difficult for the Democratic leaders in Congress to deliver sufficient votes to pass the bill. Second, the content of his message was almost too shrewd. Although everyone knew that the true reason for the projected reform was as a consequence of the conservative bias of the court, he suggested that the reform was actually intended to address its inefficiency, and the supposed incapacity of the older judges – thus alienating, amongst others, one of the foremost reformers on the Court, Louis Brandeis, who was 80. Using these two arguments as his basis, he suggested that if a federal judge who had served for at least ten years had not resigned six months after his 70th birthday, the president might be empowered to add a new judge to the bench, up to a total of not more than six new judges to the Supreme Court and 44 other judges to lower federal courts. The average age of the Supreme Court justices was 71.

The proposed judiciary bill soon ran into considerable

difficulties. Within Congress, conservatives in both parties, together with a number of pro-New Deal liberals, such as Burton Wheeler, expressed their forceful opposition. For some, the issue simply represented an opportunity to express existing hostility to the New Deal. But others were genuinely concerned at the constitutional implications of such a plan. The Chief Justice, Charles Evans Hughes, was able to illustrate that the plan as it stood would not in fact improve efficiency, thus undermining FDR's own justifications for the proposals. As for the public, whilst opinion was mixed, many Americans believed (erroneously) that the number of judges was prescribed by the Constitution. With so many examples of dictatorship in Europe, some suggested that Roosevelt's attempts to meddle with the prized constitution indicated dictatorial ambitions on his part too. Roosevelt was unable to mobilize public opinion in his support. Meanwhile, the Court itself diverted the force of public criticism by the well-known 'switch in time that saved nine'. A number of decisions were handed down which found in favour of New Deal measures, including the Wagner Act, the Social Security Act and a Washington minimum wage law. In May 1937 one of the conservative judges, Justice Van Devanter, resigned, enabling FDR to appoint Senator Hugo Black, a liberal. With no need now for reform, the Democratic leaders in Congress could not muster sufficient support and FDR was finally forced, in July, to withdraw the proposed plan.

Franklin Roosevelt's struggle to reform the Supreme Court must count as one of his major political failures. Some have argued that, on the contrary, it was a resounding success; that FDR lost the battle but won the war. Within three years, he was able to name five of his own men to the Court, which thereafter supported federal intervention in socio-economic matters, the rights of minorities and other liberal measures. However, as against that, Roosevelt had achieved virtually nothing in the first congressional session, apart from such comparatively minor measures as the Farm Tenant Act and a National Housing Act. The abortive court fight had allowed the effective mobilization of conservative opposition, which continued to hinder further New Deal legislation. In the second half of his second term, any president is traditionally viewed as increasingly marginal, a 'lame duck'. FDR's best chance of taking the initiative had been in the first year of his second term and he had frittered it away. Looking at the rapidity with which the New Deal reform programme ran out of steam, the failure of the promises of the second inaugural speech to materialize, then it must be concluded that while he might have won the battle, the war – the war against poverty, against deprivation, on behalf of the one third of the nation ill housed, ill fed, ill clothed – had been lost.

The Supreme Court battle had destroyed some of Roosevelt's popularity with the public. This growing sense of disillusionment was heightened by other developments which made support for further reform unlikely. Sit-down strikes, paralysing a number of industries but notably the automobile industry, raised severe doubts in many Americans' minds about the value of supporting labour. And towards the end of the year a severe economic recession cast doubts upon the President's economic policies. This recession could hardly be blamed upon the previous Republican administration, nor was there any obvious world cause. FDR was thus caught in a trap largely of his own making; by delaying further reform until he had dealt with the Supreme Court, he allowed the recession and labour unrest, both seen as the results of his earlier policies, to reduce his support. At one level, he was perhaps fortunate that international affairs offered him another stage on which to shine. Yet even here, there were problems; at the same time as Roosevelt was attempting in vain to push through reform legislation, he was also fighting with Congress over the neutrality laws.

During the 1930s, membership of trade unions within the United States increased, not least as a result of section 7(a) of the NIRA, which enabled labour leaders such as John Lewis to argue (misleadingly) that 'Your President wants you to join a union.' In 1935 the Wagner Act had provided federal guarantees of collective bargaining. In this improved atmosphere, unionization had spread to the vital mass-production industries, such as steel and automobiles. It must be emphasized that these developments did not represent any deeply held views of Roosevelt himself, who showed no signs of supporting the idea of collective bargaining as such and whose views on labour were strongly paternalistic. His appointment as Secretary of Labour, Frances Perkins, was a departure from the normal pattern (which was to appoint a unionist) and showed that it was the welfare and reform elements of the Labour Department, rather than those concerned with the unions, which most concerned the President. However, the gains made by unions took place during the Roosevelt administration, labour benefited from the reform and anti-business atmosphere of the New Deal, whilst the attitude of those within the administration was that labour unions should not be discriminated against.

In the immediate aftermath of the Wagner Act, unions had still to fight for their position, as many employers initially refused to abide by its provisions. Meanwhile, industrial unions flourished, and in November 1935 they formed the Committee (later Congress) of Industrial Organization. The new unions achieved considerable success. In December 1936 there was a strike at General Motors in Flint, which saw the use of the sit-down strike, in which factories were occupied to prevent the use of strike breakers. General Motors surrendered after six weeks. In March 1937 US Steel gave way without a fight, granting union recognition, increased wages and a 40-hour week. Union membership soared, from four million members in 1936 to seven million in 1937. Most of these new members went into the CIO, whose leaders favoured the augmentation of their industrial power with favourable legislation. The organization also favoured social welfare legislation, on the lines of the Social Security Act. In other words, they regarded political activity as justified, and indeed necessary. Following the Second Hundred Days in particular, FDR was clearly the most sympathetic of the likely presidential contenders and in 1936 he had been given the overt support of the Labour Non-Partisan League.

This labour support however meant that FDR was tarred with the same brush as the labour leaders in the eyes of the public and particularly of businessmen. As union leaders became more aggressive in their approach to industrial relations, their support became more of a handicap than a help to the President. This was particularly true following the rash of strikes, especially sit-down strikes, in the winter of 1936–7. Business expected him to protect their property by sending in the federal troops, an action which he was unprepared to take. Labour expected him to support their position, but this was something that he could not afford to do either. Although doing nothing was his best option, given the circumstances, it earned him the distrust of both sides, whilst many Americans unassociated with the industrial conflicts themselves were very concerned by the potential threat to property and saw the sit-down strikes as incredibly dangerous radicalism.

Roosevelt had thus managed to alienate many of the American people, either unwittingly, as in the case of labour, or through his deliberate pursuit of his Supreme Court policy. This alienation was exacerbated by another factor, the economic recession of 1937, which took from the President the reputation of someone who, however slowly, was solving the economic problems. FDR had claimed that the recovery had been carefully structured

71

and planned; thus the implication was bound to be that he must bear the blame for the economic recession which began in the summer of 1937. In the previous year, it had appeared as though the good times were really beginning to return, with unemployment for example coming down to under eight million, but it rapidly became evident that this was a false hope, engendered by high levels of public spending. The economy was actually marked by continuing signs of weakness such as the sluggish construction industry and mass unemployment. Nevertheless in June 1937 Roosevelt slashed public spending sharply, in line with his inherent belief that deficit spending was intrinsically wrong and could only be justified by emergency conditions. At the same time, the first social security taxes were being collected, thus taking money out of the economy. Meanwhile, the business investment that FDR had expected to take the place of public spending failed to materialize and by August 1937 industrial activity and the price of stocks, two very important indices of business confidence, had plunged downward. There was, over that summer, a return of misery and want on a scale unknown since 1932, with unemployment once again exceeding ten million.

In deciding how to deal with this recession, a split rapidly developed within the cabinet, with Roosevelt initially supporting those who maintained that the right policy was one of seeking a balanced budget through further cuts in government spending. On the other side there was a strong group calling for increased spending to buy the country out of the recession, including Harry Hopkins. Roosevelt finally sided with the latter group and in 1938 a very large sum was appropriated for relief and economic pump-priming. With this clear commitment to deficit spending, the slow path back to economic prosperity began, to reach its height in the emergency expenditures of the war years. Gradually the economic indices began to rise again, but in 1939 there were still over nine million men unemployed. It required the massive demands of American rearmament and European arms purchases for the economy to recover full prosperity, during the Second World War. FDR could never really claim that he had satisfactorily solved the problems of depression.

With all these distractions, any opportunities for long-term reform were obviously diminished. Moreover, in planning his future strategy, Roosevelt had also to consider the situation prevailing in Congress, for to propose legislation only to have it rejected would, especially in the light of the Supreme Court fiasco, considerably diminish his reputation. In both 1937 and 1938 this situation was to arise. Prior to 1937 it had been very difficult for Democrats to express opposition to Roosevelt, in view of his immense popularity. However, thereafter elements within the party began to oppose his proposals, including the Vice President, John Garner. Many prominent Democrats were already looking to the 1940 convention, when it was assumed that a new presidential candidate would have to be chosen. They resented the domination of the New Deal bureaucrats and hoped to have a greater party representation in any future administration. This intransigence within Congress, beginning at the time of the court plan and growing thereafter, did much to bring about the demise of the New Deal.

To sum up, the legislative accomplishments of 1937 and 1938 were slight, both in comparison with the major measures of the first term and with FDR's own rhetorical aspirations. In 1937, he managed to push through farm tenancy and housing acts, but lacking adequate appropriations, their impact was limited. Also a large-scale programme of slum clearance and public housing to address the problem of the 'ill-housed' third of a nation was never put into action. In November therefore, he decided to repeat a strategy which had been successful two years previously. He called a special session and demanded a number of 'must' measures, including a maximum hours, minimum wage act, an act to reorganize the executive branch and the creation of seven little TVAs. This strategy had worked in 1935, but then he had been dealing with a more radical Congress. Now, his attempt to seize the political initiative was only partially successful, and none of the measures were passed in their intended form. Despite these failures, in 1938 a large appropriation was secured, a Temporary National Economic Committee was created to launch a campaign against monopolistic big business and a new agricultural act, which promoted the idea of an 'ever normal granary' was passed. In addition, the FLSA was passed, enforcing important measures on minimum wages, maximum hours and the prohibition of child labour. However, the scope of this act was considerably reduced by Congress, a proposed tax act was mutilated and executive reorganization was rejected. Congress had thus supported the measures likely to win popular support so necessary in an election year, yet also asserted their independence. Roosevelt meanwhile had consolidated some of his earlier programmes, but had introduced little that was new.

In pursuing his fight with the legislature, Roosevelt managed to alienate a powerful group within his own party. The desire of the President to appear above party, to win the support of bipartisan liberal progressive sentiment within the United States, was unlikely to appeal to many conservative Democrats. This led to the fear that the progressive mantle might be wrested from him, particularly when in April 1938 Governor Philip La Follette of Wisconsin launched a new party, the National Progressives of America. Faced with growing resistance and conservatism within his own party, FDR was determined to use the 1938 mid-term elections, to 'purge' the Democratic party of some of its more reactionary elements. He tried to achieve this by the use of patronage and the

encouragement of internal party challenges to his opponents. However, yet again his political judgement was at
fault. He was entering into what most contemporaries
regarded as his 'lame-duck' period, a time when his
authority over his party was more likely to decline, than
expand. Moreover, most of the conservatives came from
the South; not only were they expressing the views of
many of their constituents, but their power bases were
well entrenched. The purge was a failure and a major
political mistake. Eleanor Roosevelt believed that if Louis
Howe had been alive, the errors might have been
avoided, for Louis would have seen the political ramific-
ations and brought them home forcibly to FDR, as Jim
Farley, despite his bitter opposition, was unable to do.
With the death of Louis in April 1936, Roosevelt had lost
an invaluable asset; not just an intensely loyal friend – he
was to find others like that, notably Harry Hopkins – but
a man who had great political shrewdness and did not
hesitate to argue with FDR if he felt his ideas were wrong.

Not only had FDR failed to purge his party, but the
1938 mid-term elections brought about the strengthening
of the conservative bloc in Congress. The Republicans
gained 81 seats in the House and eight seats in Senate;
they also won control of an additional 13 state governor-
ships. Within the Democratic party, the position of the
Southern conservatives had been strengthened. Thereafter, little could be achieved and to all intents and
purposes the New Deal was over. The only remaining
achievement was the passage, in 1939, of the Executive
Reorganization Act, albeit with a number of amendments.
This measure set up an Executive Office to provide the
required administrative support of the Presidency. The
Bureau of the Budget was placed under its aegis and,
under later presidents, the Office was to become the
location of the National Security Council and the Central
Intelligence Agency. Roosevelt had thus set the scene for
the modern presidency, in the sense of a carefully

co-ordinated and structured executive, able to provide the centralized direction appropriate to a federal government which was now engaged in a vastly expanded group of activities, including a greater direction of the economy, a new role in welfare, and, ultimately, a much stronger foreign policy. The legislation formalized a trend clearly apparent during FDR's presidency, for the conduct of government to become far more concentrated in the presidential office. However, important as this measure was in the long term, it was no substitute for fundamental social reform or economic restructuring.

Despite the sweeping mandate of 1936, therefore, little had been achieved in the second term, although much still remained to be done. This is not as surprising as it might appear, for having once allowed a conservative coalition to build up as a consequence of the failures of strategy over the Supreme Court battle, Roosevelt was too much the realist to fight a battle that was already lost. According to James Burns, FDR was both a lion and a fox – 'One must therefore be a fox to recognize traps and a lion to frighten wolves ...'[8] Roosevelt now allowed the fox to predominate. Attempts were made to introduce reforms, the special session represented a change in strategy, but basically, once those and the attempted purge had failed, there was little to be gained from a continued effort to introduce reform. Moreover, there is no sign that Roosevelt had a strong reform programme which he was eager to implement. The Second Hundred Days, especially the Social Security Act, represented the main thrust of his reforming instincts. Although he had responded to pressure from more radically inclined New Dealers, they too were disheartened by the troubles of the second term. New Left historians, such as Conkin, see in this failure to implement more far reaching changes the tragedy of the New Deal: '... the story of the New Deal is a sad story, the ever-recurring story of what might have been'.[9] But Roosevelt, and, it is probably true to say, the vast majority of the American people, did not want to see a completely altered socio-economic structure. There were faults in the New Deal, no doubt, it had been cut short when there still remained much to be done, but any challenge to the established patterns of authority or the private enterprise system would have met with little support.

Roosevelt still retained the loyal support of the under-privileged who, despite the frustrations experienced by the administration, were seeing the concrete gains of the first term in the social security provisions, the assistance for collective bargaining and large-scale public works and relief. The significance of this, of the sense of hope generated by the WPA schemes, of the various rural reform measures, should not be underestimated. This is apparent in the later recollections of the Americans who experienced the schemes. 'The NYA (National Youth Administration) was my salvation ... I could just as easily have been in Sing Sing as with the UN,' commented one UNICEF administrator. A child of the Depression remem-bered '... my father immediately got employed in the WPA. This was a godsend. This was the greatest thing. It meant food, you know. Survival, just survival.'[10] More-over, to a large extent it was Roosevelt personally who was seen as responsible for the assistance given to so many Americans. This goes some way to explaining why, despite the failures and concerns of the second term, he secured an unprecedented third election victory in 1940. However, of great importance also were the concurrent developments in foreign policy, which offered Roosevelt an opportunity to recapture the initiative. His 1939 State of the Union message was almost entirely concerned with foreign affairs. With his ability to relate foreign policy to the feelings of many Americans, he recaptured much of the support he had lost with the errors of his domestic policy, enabling him to be re-elected for an unprece-dented third term.

The Internationalist as Isolationist, 1933–41

5

At least until the troubled years of the Cold War, international issues were only rarely of significance in American elections. Hence there was little incentive for politicians to be acquainted with foreign affairs. To some extent, FDR was an exception to this rule. His outlook and upbringing were considerably more cosmopolitan than those of most American presidents. By inclination, he was a Wilsonian, believing in collective security and the League of Nations and he had fought the 1920 election as an internationalist. His own background and beliefs are important for, like many presidents, Roosevelt was to determine his own foreign policy to a large degree, often bypassing the State Department and the long-suffering Secretary of State, Cordell Hull. In one vital respect, however, FDR was typical of virtually every American president; he shared the need to take heed of public opinion. To an amazing extent, American foreign policy was shaped by public opinion and the activities of a small number of vociferous lobbies. Throughout the 1930s, the debate as to how the United States should respond to the escalating tension in Europe and the Far East preoccupied many Americans, and particularly Congress. In evolving his foreign policy, FDR had constantly to consider the strength of popular feeling within the country.

Roosevelt brought to the presidency a considerable legacy, in some respects contradictory, upon which to draw. His orientation was clearly towards Europe, although his years at the Navy Department had convinced him of the importance of Japan for the security of the United States. At this early stage in his career, FDR had appeared to be an advocate of the kind of paternalistic imperialism represented by his distant cousin Theodore. He believed that armed intervention was justified if law and order, improvements in health and education, and democracy followed. It may well be that in his support for the League of Nations, he began to move away from these earlier opinions. Even so, during the 1920 presidential campaign, he had claimed that the United States effectively controlled several Central American republics and that he had been personally responsible for the writing of Haiti's constitution. Yet in his adherence to the League and his rejection of out and out isolationism, he seems to have been expressing a personally held opinion, rather than simply following his party's line. During the 1920s he took the lead in setting up the Woodrow Wilson Foundation and encouraged the study of international relations in American universities. Although he accepted that the United States was never likely to join the League, he nonetheless hoped that a brand new organization might be set up to which it could adhere.

By 1928, his ideas on foreign affairs were beginning to crystallize. In contradiction to his own earlier beliefs, he disapproved of the armed intervention by marines in Nicaragua. In an article written in 1928 for the prestigious journal, *Foreign Affairs*, he urged the desirability of international co-operation, although he was ambivalent about the League and the World Court. This ambivalence was politically shrewd, particularly in the early 1930s, when international responses to the Manchurian crisis re-opened the whole question of collective security. As Governor of New York, Roosevelt was not called upon to pronounce on foreign affairs and could argue that, as a state governor, it was inappropriate for him to speak on national issues. During the 1932 election campaign, he could no longer maintain this position. Nonetheless he said little about foreign affairs, even agreeing not to pursue American membership of the League or the World Court in order to secure the support of William Randolph Hearst. The American people therefore probably had little idea about the views of their new President on world affairs – views which were, however, akin to those of the previous Republican administration on several key issues. Indeed, during the interregnum, the president-elect issued a statement supporting Henry Stimson's non-recognition doctrine, evolved in order to respond to the Japanese occupation of Manchuria.

Nor were foreign affairs pressing when the time came for Roosevelt to assume the Presidency. In his first inau-gural speech, the new President had little to say about international matters. His preoccupation, like that of the rest of the American people, was with the devastating economic crisis. About the only reference he made to the world outside the United States came in a sentence dedi-cating himself to the policy of the 'good neighbour'. Although in the speech no definition of area was given, the phrase has been traditionally associated with his policy towards Latin America, a region of particular importance to the United States. To understand why that is so, it is necessary to examine the history of American relations with the region.

In the early 20th century the United States had followed an interventionist policy towards Central America and the Caribbean, in part to deter possible European involvement. Central America in particular was vital strategically to the United States; there must be no threat to safe passage through the Panama Canal, without which the naval forces of the United States would be considerably reduced in effectiveness. During his time as Assistant Secretary of the Navy, FDR had actively participated in Wilson's interventionism and thus one would expect him to follow a similar policy during his own presidency. However, the situation in Latin America was changing, a fact reflected in the policies of the Hoover administration. The likelihood of European intervention in the region was now very slim, while the more powerful nations in South America, notably Argentina, Brazil and Chile, did not take kindly to manifestations of what they saw as Yankee imperialism. During the 1920s, the pattern of investment within Latin America generally and specifically Central America had turned very much towards the United States. The Americans now dominated by virtue of economic power; they had no need to use military coercion. Indeed, the retention of an overtly interventionist policy was not just unnecessary, it was actually counter-productive.

Whilst FDR did not initiate a new departure in American policy towards the rest of the hemisphere, he did use his powers of rhetoric to emphasize the 'good neighbour' approach far more than Hoover had done and so won for himself considerable support within Latin America. In the first year of the administration, at a Pan-American conference in Montevideo, Secretary of State Hull supported the proposition that no state had the right to intervene in the affairs of another. Later that year, when trouble flared in Cuba, FDR chose not to interfere militarily, although he did have naval vessels standing nearby, in case of need. He even formally repudiated the Platt Amendment, under which the United States was granted considerable powers of intervention in Cuba. In 1936 the president made a long visit to the region, taking in several different states and stressing his policy of conciliation. Increasingly, he stressed the importance of Pan-American co-operation on matters of concern to the hemisphere.

An interesting reflection of Roosevelt's pursuit of the 'good neighbour' policy came in Mexico. While in the Navy Department, Roosevelt had supported an interventionist response to Mexican infringements of American rights and at one point appeared to be advocating war. As President, he had to face a similar crisis, when in 1938 the Mexican Government expropriated American oil companies. On this occasion, however, he was to adopt a considerably more conciliatory approach, aided by his pacifist ex-chief, Josephus Daniels. Although economic sanctions were taken against Mexico, they were far less severe than either the oil companies or the State Department wished. Great Britain broke off diplomatic relations with Mexico, an example which the United States did not follow. As Mexico showed signs of developing economic links with Germany, the Roosevelt administration became ever more concerned. Admittedly, it was not until the Second World War broke out, that the US Government finally accepted a compromise settlement. However, throughout the crisis, by following a conciliatory policy, Roosevelt ensured that relations with the USA's closest neighbour were not ruptured.

A more conciliatory policy towards the rest of the hemisphere also promised to be economically rewarding. A major factor in the world crisis of the 1930s was the steady drift into economic nationalism which considerably reduced the volume of international trade. One response to this, strongly advocated by Secretary of State Cordell Hull, was the negotiation of bilateral trade treaties by which the United States and the other party would promise to reduce duties reciprocally. Latin America was an area where such negotiations might well be profitable, capitalizing upon a region that was within the economic sphere of influence of the United States. A number of such treaties were in fact signed during the 1930s, though their economic impact was somewhat less than hoped. Meanwhile, by the late 1930s, there was an additional reason to emphasize hemispheric solidarity in the face of growing tension and fascist sentiment in Europe and the Far East. In such a troubled world, it was important to retain the support of the Latin American countries, not least those whose own regimes showed fascist tendencies. When war broke out, the American nations acted together to formulate neutrality policies, in an attempt to isolate the hemisphere from the adverse effects of war.

It is therefore possible to trace a consistent policy towards Latin America throughout Roosevelt's presidency, even if the reasons for being a 'good neighbour' changed through the decade. Elsewhere, however, his foreign policy had to adapt itself to rapidly changing circumstances. For his first term, it was necessarily subordinate to the pressing needs of domestic recovery. However, the two could not be so easily separated. Whether or not FDR wished to divorce the USA as far as possible from the world economy – and the signs are that, on the whole, that is just what he did want – there were aspects of American economic recovery, such as foreign trade, which could not be approached purely in isolation. Economic underpinnings to the 'good neighbour' policy were very important, while recognition of the Soviet Union in November 1933 was motivated in part by a desire to cultivate trade. And right from the very beginning of his presidency, FDR was faced by one major question – was his approach to economic recovery going to be internationalist or nationalist? He had to formulate policies on such key issues as the war debts, the gold standard and tariffs. During the interregnum, President Hoover had attempted to pin FDR down on these matters, but without success. Throughout those critical four months, the US administration was effectively stalemated.

It had already been decided to hold an international economic conference in London during June 1933 to discuss these matters multilaterally and the uncertainty concerning the new President's intentions considerably hindered preparations for the conference.

This meant that whilst promoting domestic measures in the First Hundred Days, Roosevelt had also to give thought to the international scene. As outlined above, his domestic strategy was basically structured around the raising of prices through the curtailment of production. Such a strategy presupposed a protected market, thus indicating that the lowering of tariffs would not be advantageous. Similarly, in April 1933 the United States was taken off the gold standard, in part to permit a series of inflationary measures. However, other industrial nations were looking to the United States, as the leading economic power, to play an important part in ending the global depression. Of particular significance was the question of the war debts, as France and Great Britain in particular felt that American insistence upon repayment should be abandoned. Great hopes were pinned upon the London Conference, therefore, where the shape of the new President's economic strategy would emerge.

The American delegation to the conference was led by Cordell Hull, well known for his internationalist views. But policy direction still rested with the President, who eventually expressed his opinions in a message to the conference, delivered in person by Raymond Moley. In this message, FDR stated that international recovery was best pursued by individual nations looking to their own domestic recovery. This effectively undermined the conference and with it hopes of an international strategy to deal with the depression. It also left unsolved the question of war debts, on which all the debtor nations with the exception of Finland were later to default. The President had thus retained his freedom of action, but in so doing had opted for a nationalist approach to international economic policy, an approach which not even the Reciprocal Trade Act of 1934 could undermine. Roosevelt therefore failed to take the international dimensions of the depression, although it should be pointed out that there is no evidence that he regarded this as a priority, domestic strategies for recovery having far more import-ance in his eyes.

Increasingly, however, international economic problems were to be replaced by more immediate poli-tical concerns. Initially, attention centred on the Far East and Japanese ambitions. Following their invasion of Manchuria, the Japanese left the League of Nations in March 1933 rather than remain to face condemnation. The League failed this first test of its collective power and will, refusing to take effective economic sanctions, in part because the United States would not commit itself to co-operate. Three years later, Japan walked out of the naval limitation talks and began to enact its policy of expansion in the Chinese mainland. On the other side of the world, in the same year as FDR had assumed the presidency, Adolf Hitler had come to power in Germany. By 1936 the international dimensions of his ambitions were becoming apparent. The march into the Rhineland, to be followed shortly afterwards by the *Anschluss* with Austria, demonstrated that his expansionist ambitions were not mere rhetoric. Meanwhile Mussolini's fascist regime, in power since 1922, began foreign escapades in Africa and civil war broke out in Spain. In 1937 the tension in the Far East escalated into all-out war between Japan and China. Whereas the outbreak of the First World War had taken everyone by surprise, the growing tension in Europe was apparent long before September 1939. So although domestic policy continued to pre-occupy FDR, he had increasingly to respond, if only in words, to the worsening situation abroad.

In viewing their President's responses to events else-where, the American people were motivated by one overriding desire; to escape at all costs the possibility of involvement in yet another European war. The strength of isolationism within the USA increased as the tension in Europe and the Far East escalated. In 1934 the Senate Munitions Committee concluded that US entry into the First World War had been a grievous mistake, brought about by the manipulations of a few unscrupulous arms dealers and financiers. When Roosevelt requested the Senate to approve American entry into the World Court in January 1935, although a majority of senators were in favour, the vote failed to muster the required two thirds majority. In the House of Representatives, as late as September 1941 isolationist sentiment was so strong that the selective service (conscription) act was extended for a further six months by a margin of only one vote – 203 votes to 202. Given that in order to finance military expansion, declare war or ratify any treaty, a president required Congressional sanction, there were clear limits to Roosevelt's freedom of manoeuvre. Meanwhile, among the public at large, the strength of opposition to the possibility of American entry into war was typified by the formation in 1940 of the America First Committee. At their height, the various pacifist groups had about 12 million active adherents. The most pressing expression of public opinion with which Roosevelt had to deal throughout his first two terms was the isolationist sentiment.

It was this sentiment which prompted the passing of a whole series of Neutrality Acts, commencing in 1935. Ironically, these had their origins in the desire of the administration to have powers which would enable them to impose a discriminatory arms embargo against aggressor nations. However, in this form the proposal was unacceptable to Congress, which instead sought to impose a mandatory arms embargo on all belligerents, whether aggressor or victim. Although apparently very similar, the differences between the two proposals raised the question of whether the United States would seek to *deter* war by collective security and selective action against aggressors, or *evade* war by hiding behind a shield of neutrality. It was to follow the latter path. In 1935 the first Neutrality Act was passed, incorporating the mandatory embargo on all belligerents. It was succeeded by a number of others, to Roosevelt's growing chagrin, as he found the president's traditional discretion in the field of foreign policy heavily curtailed.

The neutrality legislation was, by and large, designed to avoid a repetition of the circumstances which were thought to have drawn the United States into the last war. Thus, in case of war there was to be an embargo on the export of arms and other implements of war to belligerents, along with a ban on loans. In addition, American vessels were prohibited from carrying munitions to nations at war and, from 1937, American citizens were forbidden to sail on belligerent vessels. In 1937, also, the 'cash and carry' provision was added to the legislation. Belligerent nations were allowed to purchase prohibited commodities (but not arms), provided they were paid for upon delivery and taken away from the United States in the buyer's ships. In their preoccupation with the past war rather than the next one, the neutrality laws failed to take sufficient account of changing circumstances. Even more unfortunate was that the acts created a feeling of aloofness and detachment from events in Europe amongst the American people.

Despite this, FDR himself was clearly concerned by the growing trend towards international aggression and, some would argue, tried to educate American public opinion to recognize the danger. However, the process of 'education' was a slow one, and the President rarely went far ahead of popular feeling, shaping his policies in response to events. During the early build-up of international tension, in the period 1935–7, Roosevelt was essentially preoccupied by domestic matters. His second inaugural speech, on 20 January 1937, made no mention of foreign affairs. However, in July 1937 the growing tension in the Far East boiled over into war. In October, therefore, Roosevelt made a key speech, the so-called 'quarantine' speech, in which he condemned war and called for the international community to 'quarantine' all aggressors. 'It seems to be unfortunately true that the epidemic of world lawlessness is spreading ... When an epidemic of physical disease starts to spread, the community approves and joins in a quarantine of the patients in order to protect the health of the community against the spread of the disease.'[1] Yet little was done to build upon his suggestion, in part as a result of a wave of concern among the American public. As economic recession bit hard in the winter of 1937–8, FDR had little attention to spare for foreign affairs.

Lacking strong support from the American people, there was little that Roosevelt could hope to achieve. However, from the spring of 1938 it became increasingly apparent to all observers that peace in Europe hung by a slim thread. The President began to urge the importance of rearmament, securing an additional $500 million defence appropriation in 1938. He also began to build a closer relationship with the British, following some years of Anglo–American tension. The symbol of these improved relations came in June 1939 when King George VI became the first reigning British sovereign to visit American soil. As well as staying at the White House, he and Queen Elizabeth spent twenty-four hours at Hyde Park for an informal visit much enjoyed by all – especially the President's mother. The visit did a great deal to increase Anglophile sentiment within the United States, especially after the outbreak of war a mere three months later.

Roosevelt also made a number of abortive attempts to promote peace. In early 1938, he proposed that an international conference be held to discuss the breaking down of trade barriers and disarmament, only to see the idea cold-shouldered by the British Prime Minister, Neville Chamberlain. The following year, in April 1939, he asked Hitler and Mussolini to promise not to attack a specified 31 nations for the following ten years. This proposal was rejected out of hand and clearly had no chance of succeeding. Roosevelt was either demonstrating a woeful naivety, or a subtle and devious attempt to educate American public opinion in the perils of dealing with dictators. However, despite his growing concern at the state of affairs in Europe, he took very little concrete action to redress the problem. In looking at the 1930s, it is the collapse of collective security in the form of the League, and the appeasement policy followed by the British and French which must bear the main responsibility for the failure to halt German aggression. However, there is no doubt that the lack of clear and decisive action by the United States and its unwillingness to commit itself to collective policies such as economic sanctions against aggressors, contributed to the slow drift to war. Whether Roosevelt could have implemented a different policy, in the face of determined isolationist opposition, is a vexed question, but his efforts to take a lead came late and were often only half-hearted. Forceful speeches directed against the fascist powers would achieve little without the will to take action should the circumstances dictate.

The coming of war to Europe in September 1939 took few by surprise. Roosevelt issued the required neutrality proclamation, but he did not ask, as Wilson had done in 1914, for Americans to remain neutral in thought as well as deed: 'Even a neutral cannot be asked to close his mind or his conscience.' His sympathies were clearly on the Allied side, as were those of the vast majority of the American people. In addition, he recognized that 'when peace has been broken anywhere, the peace of all countries everywhere is in danger'.[2] FDR realized that the

Royal Navy was an important element in the preservation of free shipping lanes and in keeping the German fleet well away from the Western hemisphere. Thus the President saw the Allies as to a large degree America's first line of defence and, if this were the case, then he could not afford to let them lose. As against this, the American people, and particularly Congress, were doubly alert for any initiative which might threaten a repetition of 1917. The difficulty, then, was to find ways of extending as much aid as possible to the Allies without in any way risking the situation whereby the USA would become slowly drawn into the war. With his usual felicity, FDR was to find a number of expedients which allowed him to do this, with the support of at least most of the American people.

One of the first devices was to amend the neutrality laws. By early November 1939 Roosevelt had secured the extension of the 'cash and carry' provision to cover armaments as well as other specified commodities. Although this was ostensibly still neutral, British control of the sea meant that only the Allies could take advantage of the American market. Hopes that the Americans would be able to confine their assistance to that permitted by 'cash and carry' faded, however, during the spring and summer of 1940. The Phoney War was replaced by blitzkrieg and, as country after country fell to the Germans – Norway, Denmark, the Low Countries and then France – it became increasingly apparent that the German threat to world peace was a truly immense one. FDR had to a large extent committed his prestige to an Allied victory by his outspoken support for their cause and the provision of large-scale material aid. Increasingly, therefore, he began to sponsor measures which were blatantly unneutral, declaring as early as June 1940 that 'We will extend to the opponents of force the material resources of this nation.'[3] There was, however, a limit to how far he was able or willing to go in his assistance to the Allies. Congress was prepared to take measures which increased the defensive capacity of the United States, in May 1940 passing a massive appropriation for rearmament and even introducing conscription in August that year. But it certainly would not have supported anything akin to a declaration of war. Nor was public opinion in favour of belligerency; according to one opinion poll taken in June 1940 82 per cent of the American people opposed entry into a European war, even though only 43 per cent of the American public believed that the Allies could win. In other words, public opinion might be in favour of growing aid to the Allies, but only aid short of war.

However, the rapidity of the German advance in Europe did lead to a growing awareness of the serious international crisis. Despite the continued reiteration of 'Fortress America' ideas by isolationists, it was increasingly recognized that the USA now faced a direct threat to her national security, a threat which at best might compel her to live a precarious self-sufficient existence within her own hemisphere and at worst might pose a threat to her even there. This was a constant theme in Roosevelt's speeches from as early as September 1939. In September 1940 the sense of threat to the United States was increased by the announcement of the Tripartite Pact between Japan, Germany and Italy. However, the task of responding to this within the constraints of public opinion was far from easy – not least because the President, too, hoped to avoid direct involvement in war. In an attempt to minimize opposition, Roosevelt emphasized the bipartisan nature of foreign policy by appointing to his cabinet two leading Republicans, Henry Stimson and Frank Knox, in the vital roles of Secretary of War and Secretary of the Navy.

In shaping his foreign policy during the critical summer months of 1940, Roosevelt had to take account both of international affairs and domestic considerations. For that was the period when the drawn-out political process involved in the choice of a president began, in preparation for the presidential election due in November. By tradition and precedent, no president had served more than two full terms. Thus, the common expectation was that FDR would step down from the presidency in January 1941. However, there was no undisputed successor to FDR within the Democratic party who could be counted upon to safeguard the New Deal legacy. Additionally, it became apparent that the new president would be faced with an immense international crisis, particularly after May 1940. Roosevelt therefore decided that he would run again, using as his justification the parlous state of affairs in Europe. He felt sufficiently strong in his own control of the party and the Democratic electorate to choose a new running mate, his Secretary of Agriculture Henry Wallace, who was a liberal from the Mid-West. In fighting for a third term, however, FDR had obviously to contend against the ingrained belief that what was right for George Washington ought to be right for him. He also had to counter charges that he wanted to remain president in order to take the USA into the European war.

These two charges were obviously central to the Republican campaign, for although that party's candidate, Wendell Willkie, was an internationalist, he was slipping badly in the polls. He was thus driven to resort to the charge that FDR was scheming to take the USA into the war. The President met this charge squarely, maintaining that 'your boys are not going to be sent into any foreign wars',[4] comments with overtones of Wilson's 1916 campaign. Like Wilson, FDR was to find his comments rang hollow only months after the election. Nonetheless, they helped him to win. Roosevelt's victory in November by 27,244,160 votes to 22,305,198 was by no means as sweeping as his landslide in 1936, but it guaranteed him a further four years in the White House. It could also be seen as a mandate for his pledge not to enter the war and meant that, at least for the foreseeable future, FDR would have to honour that commitment. The British had hoped that, with the election over, the USA might contemplate belligerency, but that was a misreading of the situation. President Roosevelt was not awaiting the chance to enter the war on the side of the Allies; he genuinely sought a means by which the United States could give the fullest assistance, without becoming involved in the fighting.

The fact still remained, however, that the British Empire was now the only bulwark against Hitler and if the British collapsed, then the United States would inexorably be drawn into the struggle. For the British, American material aid was critical, a point well appreciated by Winston Churchill, who had become Prime Minister in May 1940. At his instigation, in August that same year FDR had used his powers as Commander-in-Chief to conclude the famous destroyers-for-bases deal, whereby in return for 50 over-age destroyers he secured 99-year leases on a number of bases in Britain's Western hemisphere possessions. However, Britain's supply position continued to worsen and by late 1940 she was no longer able to fetch American goods on a 'cash and carry' basis. Over the next few months, little by little, the remaining provisions of the neutrality laws were scrapped. On the financial side, Roosevelt proposed a measure which was to be hailed as a major step in the fight for freedom by Great Britain – Lend Lease.

Only proposed in December 1940, a month after his re-election, Lend Lease provided a means of supplying the British war effort, whilst avoiding the rancour and difficulties caused by the war debts of the Great War. The President was authorized to provide armaments to any country whose defence he regarded as vital to the national security of the United States; after the end of the war, the recipient would be expected to return the goods in kind. As he was so often to do, FDR explained the scheme to the American public by the use of a homely analogy; the neighbour who, seeing his neighbour's house on fire, lent his hose to help put out the flames. He wasn't interested in being paid for the hose, but in receiving back at the end of the emergency either his own hose or another one in return. Implicit in the analogy was the fear that if the neighbour did not put out the flames the conflagration might spread to his own property. For Britain, with very low financial reserves, this was a vital lifeline. On 30 December 1940 FDR gave a fireside chat to the American people, in which he declared his intention to give all aid to Great Britain short of war. Pointing out that if Great Britain were defeated, 'all of us, in all the Americas, would be living at the point of a gun', he went on to declare that 'we must be the great arsenal of democracy. For us this is an emergency as serious as war itself.'[5]

However, tellingly, the Lend Lease bill had a tough ride through Congress, even though it was justified on the grounds that by becoming the arsenal of democracy, the United States would save itself from having to fight. Roosevelt still had a long way to go in the task of 'educating' the American public, even in his limited vision of the appropriate role for the USA. In January 1941 FDR tried to commit the American people to the ideological fight against fascism by presenting his own views of what the war was about. The Four Freedoms speech, delivered on 6 January 1941, emphasized the importance of freedom of speech, freedom of religion, freedom from fear and freedom from want. American propaganda throughout the war was based upon this concept of the 'Four Freedoms'. This task of giving the war an American relevance was taken one step further in the Atlantic Charter – a list of post-war priorities agreed by President Roosevelt and Churchill in August 1941. The Charter was a result of the meeting off Newfoundland between Roosevelt and Churchill and was aimed, on the American side, at removing any fears that the cynical old world would simply use the United States to fight in order to preserve the status quo. It contained commitments to the freedom of the seas, sovereign rights and self-government for all peoples, opposition to imposed or undemocratic territorial changes and increased international economic opportunity. Once the United States became a belligerent, later adherents to the alliance were asked to accept the basic principles of the Atlantic Charter, thus hypothetically eliminating any possibility of disagreement over war aims.

Once Lend Lease was in operation, Roosevelt was able to use his discretionary powers to give considerable aid to Great Britain and, after October 1941, the Soviet Union, which had been invaded by the German Army some months earlier. Assistance was also given to the Chinese, under fierce attack by the Japanese. As the level of American aid departed further and further from the strict spirit of neutrality, it seemed ever more likely that, despite all Roosevelt's efforts, the United States would become a belligerent in due course. However, he devoted much care and attention to the increasingly difficult task of walking the tightrope of neutrality. Nowhere was this more apparent than in his handling of events on the other side of the world, in the Far East. It is important to remember that in these years tension was escalating in the Pacific as well as in Europe. For many in the United States, it was events in the Far East, rather than Europe, which appeared the more threatening. To understand why, it is necessary to understand the particular significance of China in the eyes of many Americans, including Roosevelt himself.

As a trans-continental, two-ocean nation, the United States had always had to take account of events in the Far East. It had been an American, Commodore Perry, who had opened up Japan to the West in 1854. However, most attention centred upon China, both for trading purposes and as the destination of a growing number of American missionaries. The 'Open Door' notes of 1899 had been drawn up in an attempt to protect American economic interests in China and, although trade did not increase to the extent that some had hoped, the sheer size of this potential market continued to fascinate American merchants. Amongst those trading with China was FDR's maternal grandfather, Warren Delano. The president had grown up surrounded by Chinese memorabilia and regaled by his grandfather with tales of his days in the China trade. The instinctive American sympathy for the Chinese was enhanced by the democratic republic established following the 1911 revolution. By the late 1920s, the nationalist regime of Chiang Kai-Shek was flawed by corruption and inefficiency, but that did not diminish American support.

Japanese–American relations were considerably less harmonious. From the Japanese point of view, the reputation of the USA was tarnished by its restrictive immigration regulations, prompted by fears of large-scale Japanese immigration to the West Coast. As for the Americans, they were concerned about the sizeable Japanese population within Hawaii and the growing Japanese naval presence in the Pacific. The United States, after all, held a number of colonial possessions within the Pacific – Guam, Wake Island and above all the Philippines. A major goal of the American delegations to all the disarmament conferences held in the inter-war years was to limit the size of Japan's navy. Talk of a Greater Asia Co-Prosperity Sphere, or of a Japanese Monroe Doctrine in the Far East alarmed the USA. Although they had failed to take really decisive action in the case of either the Manchurian crisis of 1931–3, or the full-scale invasion of China by Japan in 1937, both President Hoover and FDR had demonstrated a high level of concern.

Nonetheless, apart from the quarantine speech of

1937, which had come to nothing, Roosevelt had consistently avoided undue involvement in the Far East, despite the growing public hostility to Japanese aggression. FDR believed that Germany posed the greater threat to American national security and was anxious not to divert attention from events in the Atlantic. Initially, too, he did not wish to do anything which might undermine the position of the moderates within the Japanese government. But by 1940 Japan's ambitions in the Pacific were expanding at the cost of the colonial possessions of the beleaguered European powers. Ironically, her war preparations were aided by American supplies, specifically scrap iron and petroleum. In seeking to respond to considerable pressure from within his cabinet to stop supplying Japan with these important commodities, Roosevelt was at pains to avoid any action which might provoke the Japanese to invade the oil-rich Dutch East Indies (modern-day Indonesia). Joint Anglo–American war plans in the second half of 1941 assumed that there would be a forward policy in the Atlantic and only a holding operation in the Pacific. Yet at the same time, events in the Far East were moving swiftly. The German attack upon the Soviet Union had removed Japan's fears of Russian reaction to her forward policies and enabled her to proceed with her advance through Indochina. Roosevelt's response was still to temporize, and continue negotiations for as long as possible, although in July 1941 economic sanctions were imposed, including an embargo on oil exports from the United States to Japan. This action increased pressure upon Japan to consolidate the Greater Asia Co-Prosperity Sphere and made a Japanese advance towards the Dutch East Indies, Singapore and eventually the Philippines more likely.

Even so, Japanese–American negotiations continued on a number of issues, including the presence of Japanese troops in China and the more general question of the status quo within the Pacific. Discussions in August and September 1941 centred upon American attempts to persuade Japan to withdraw her troops from China and Indochina in return for commercial benefits. The failure to reach an agreement contributed to the replacement of Japanese Prime Minister Prince Konoye by the hard-line General Tojo. Despite this, negotiations continued right up until the eve of Pearl Harbor, although it is doubtful whether any accord was likely between Japan, determined to implement her economic and political ambitions in the Far East, and the United States, to whom such goals were anathema. Japanese war preparations continued regardless, a fact well known to the Americans, who had already cracked the secret Japanese communications code. Historical opinion varies as to the extent to which either side took the negotiations seriously. However, suggestions that Roosevelt actually sought to antagonize Japan in order to provoke an attack on the USA, so as to enter the war 'through the back door', fail to take into account the overall context and direction of his policies.[6] Although he was unprepared to compromise to the extent of accepting Japanese incursions in China and Indochina, he certainly did not want to see the United States at war in the Pacific, particularly if it was still at peace in the Atlantic.

Meanwhile, on the European front, to which Roosevelt assigned the first priority, he acted to relieve the British of as much routine military activity as possible. In April 1941 FDR announced that the US Navy would extend its Atlantic patrol area as far East as the 25th meridian and at the end of May the Americans took over from the British the military and air bases in Iceland. The following month FDR agreed to establish a ferry service across the Atlantic from Brazil to West Africa, using American army pilots. Although in June 1941 the war was transformed with the invasion of the Soviet Union by Hitler, the steady escalation of aid continued, with the Soviet Union eventually a recipient as well as Great

Britain. In August came the Newfoundland meeting between Roosevelt and Churchill, at which the President led the British to believe that American entry into the war was merely a matter of time, arguing that he was simply awaiting a suitable incident. Although it is hard to be sure at what point FDR became convinced that American belligerency was inevitable – and he may still have hoped to avoid outright involvement in a shooting war – for the last six months of 1941 British and American army staffs were pooling high-level intelligence and preparing war plans ready for the contingency of American entry into the war. From September US naval vessels were attacking German warships on sight, a policy which Roosevelt justified on the basis that 'when you see a rattlesnake poised to strike, you do not wait until he has struck before you crush him.'[7] In mid-November, the neutrality acts were fully amended, allowing US merchant ships to be armed. To all intents and purposes, therefore, the United States and Germany were conducting a naval war in the Atlantic, although it was not acknowledged as such by either side.

Throughout this period, more and more arms were made available to the British, despite the possible adverse consequences upon the rearmament programme under way for the US services. There were some positive spin-offs however. As well as encouraging the expansion of armament factories, the booming employment which resulted brought the Depression to an end. Though the Battle of the Atlantic resulted in a grievous loss of vessels, the President did all that he could to ensure that American supplies reached their ultimate destinations. He also sent special missions to Great Britain to improve communications and understanding, the first headed by his most trusted aide, Harry Hopkins. Despite all this, however, the United States was still not a belligerent and when on 31 October 1941 the American destroyer *Reuben James* was torpedoed in the North Atlantic while escorting a British convoy, it did not lead to a declaration of war. However much FDR assured the British that he wished to enter the war and was simply awaiting an incident to convince the American people, yet as the first year of Roosevelt's unprecedented third term drew to its close, he still continued his delicate balancing act between neutrality and belligerency, responding to events as and when they came.

However, in the Far East, Japan was no longer willing to hold back on her plans for empire, even though this would inevitably mean conflict with the United States. The precarious stalemate was finally resolved by Japanese action, when on 7 December 1941 – 'a date which will live in infamy'[8] – in a surprise attack Japanese planes bombed the American fleet at anchor in Pearl Harbor, Hawaii. It was not until some hours after the attack that the Japanese ultimatum was delivered to the State Department. The following day, Congress declared that the USA and Japan were at war. The dilemma of whether to enter the European war as well was solved when on 11 December the other two members of the Tripartite Pact, Germany and Italy, announced that they were at war with the United States. With the Japanese action, the nature of the Second World War had been transformed. 'Today all of us are in the same boat with you and the people of the Empire,' Roosevelt cabled to Winston Churchill on 8 December, 'and it is a ship which will not and cannot be sunk.'[9]

Roosevelt the International Statesman, 1941–45

6

The United States remained at war until the surrender of Japan in August 1945, a period of nearly four years. Throughout that time, until his own death on 12 April 1945, Roosevelt remained in the White House. With the coming of war, his work load and the strains upon him increased tremendously. Domestically, he had to direct the transformation of the economy and government apparatus to cope with the demands of total war. In addition, his military duties as Commander-in-Chief demanded constant attention. Although FDR placed considerable trust in his generals and his chiefs of staff, it was he who had to reconcile strategic priorities with political goals. He did not hesitate to impose his own opinions in questions of military strategy; his interest in geopolitics, together with his experience with the Navy during the First World War, lent him considerable self-assurance. In addition to his enhanced domestic role, his international significance increased dramatically, as he became a powerful member of the triumvirate directing the strategy of the Grand Alliance and planning the post-war world. For the last four years of his life, Roosevelt was truly a figure of global importance.

He was also, to a large degree, the main determinant of American policy and strategy. Civilian cabinet members saw less of the President as his time was increasingly occupied by the service chiefs. It is noticeable that whereas in Great Britain a small 'war cabinet' of senior politicians was formed, in the USA there was no such group. Roosevelt continued to conduct much of his own foreign policy; Secretary of State Hull did not even attend all of the wartime Big Three conferences, whilst FDR tended to rely upon special missions by his own men (such as Harry Hopkins) rather than the established diplomatic network. Hopkins was quickly acknowledged as Roosevelt's right hand man, well aware of the President's views and able to speak for him with authority. However, later in the war Hopkins' severe illness impaired his effectiveness. As during the New Deal years, competitive administration in wartime diplomacy caused considerable confusion and duplication, but it left the ultimate authority in the President's own hands. Moreover, as during all wars, the role of Congress declined, not only in the areas of military and foreign policy, but even in domestic matters, where the paramount demands of national unity during war made sustained or bitter opposition difficult to justify. To a considerable degree, therefore, the policies of the USA during the Second World War – together with their contradictions and uncertainties – were those of President Roosevelt.

In the days after Pearl Harbor, the President's first task was clearly to determine how best the USA could contribute to the war effort already being waged by Great Britain and the Soviet Union. There were a number of options; the USA might, for example, continue to emphasize its role as a major producer of critical war supplies, rather than as a source of manpower. This would enable Roosevelt to fulfil one of his key goals – to minimize American losses in the battlefield. On the other hand, the other Allied powers had already suffered major losses, especially the Soviet Union. FDR had also to decide whether to remain aloof from the other belligerents, as Wilson had done during the First World War; or accept, contrary to American tradition, an alliance with the other powers fighting the Axis. Although reluctant to accept Churchill's dream of a 'Grand Alliance', which might necessitate congressional approval, FDR did not wish to insist upon a distinct role as an 'associate'. Instead he proposed that all the nations fighting the Axis powers should be termed the 'United Nations'. On 1 January 1942 the United States, Great Britain, the Soviet Union, China and some twenty-two other nations issued a declaration in which they subscribed to the principles of the Atlantic Charter and promised not to make a separate peace. Thus, the USA was firmly bound to its allies in the fight against fascism.

Even before this, however, Roosevelt had to decide how best to utilize American forces in the first months of the war. Although a biography of Roosevelt is not the place to provide a detailed account of military strategy during the war, neither must it be forgotten that Roosevelt's own tight control over both strategy and post-war planning meant that his views and policies played a vital part in shaping key decisions. It might appear that having entered the war against Germany, Italy and Japan, the difficulties associated with wanting to assist the Allies were over; but this was far from being the case. FDR personally favoured the 'Atlantic First' policy, based upon the assumption that Germany was the main enemy, and that only when she had been defeated would it be possible to turn full attention to Japan. However, there were a great many people in the United States, and indeed within the services, who saw no reason for such an order of priorities, preferring rather to concentrate upon the Pacific. Such an argument was buttressed by the disastrous course of the war in the Far East during the first half of 1942, as Guam, Wake Island, the

Philippines – all American possesions – and also Malaya, Borneo and Singapore fell to the Japanese.

Despite this pressure, FDR remained convinced by the 'Atlantic First' strategy. In this he was aided by the persuasion of Winston Churchill, who was so anxious to gain American support in Europe that he paid an almost immediate visit to Washington D.C., spending Christmas 1941 in the White House. He spent three weeks there, during which time the two leaders not only discussed strategy, but also took the first steps towards creating a personal friendship. A united Anglo-American command structure was set up and it was also agreed that the Atlantic theatre of the war was the decisive one. Roosevelt made it plain that American soldiers would be thrown quickly into the battle against European fascism, with plans for the first US troops to reach Great Britain within weeks.

However, as 1942 progressed, the question arose as to how best to utilize the new input of manpower. Roosevelt was initially anxious to launch an attack upon the mainland of Western Europe. Churchill was more cautious, stressing the desirability of first a North African campaign and then an assault upon Italy. At British instigation, the Americans abandoned any thoughts of a cross-Channel invasion in 1942 (or even 1943). However, Roosevelt was keen that American troops should engage the enemy quickly and with a good chance of a rapid victory. During the first half of 1942, therefore, FDR agreed with the plan to invade Algeria and Morocco (the so-called 'Torch' offensive) to relieve pressure on the British in North Africa. The President even overruled his own Joint Chiefs of Staff in order to push this through. In November 1942, American troops landed in North Africa, and made rapid inroads into Vichy-held French territory there. During the winter of 1942–3, the tide began to turn in favour of the Allies on a number of fronts.

Yet, having agreed to the North African strategy, it was

hard to resist British arguments that the best way of building upon the victories in the Middle East and Africa was to consolidate the Allied hold on the Mediterranean by an attack on Italy during 1943. This, however, postponed the cross-Channel invasion yet again and increased Stalin's doubts about the ultimate intentions of his allies. Russian troops continued to bear the brunt of the German onslaught throughout 1942 and 1943. On the other hand, Churchill's success in postponing the opening of a Second Front did enable the diversion of some American troops to the Pacific, thus helping to answer critics of the 'Atlantic First' strategy. After the American victory at the Battle of Midway (June 1942), there was a switch to the offensive in the Pacific war, reinforced by the Battle of Guadalcanal in mid-November. At points, up to a third of American troops engaged overseas were fighting in the Pacific.

During 1942 and indeed for much of 1943, Roosevelt tended to follow British initiatives, sometimes in the face of opposition from his own Chiefs of Staff. At their meeting at Casablanca in January 1943, Churchill was the politically dominant partner, securing the President's approval of British strategy. Roosevelt's main contribution was an insistence that fighting would continue until the unconditional surrender of the Axis powers. However, gradually FDR began to assert himself against his British ally, while the American Chiefs of Staff became more used to operating as a unit, in order to ensure that American wishes prevailed. By the end of 1943, Roosevelt and his military staff were adamant that Anglo-American troops must engage German troops in Western Europe by the early summer of 1944 and at the Teheran conference in December 1943 Churchill was reluctantly compelled to accede to the plan for 'Overlord'. This decision represented the transfer of superior political influence to the United States, which already dominated in terms of military fighting power.

By 1944 Germany was on the defensive, although it was not until May 1945 that victory in Europe was secured. In January 1944 – six months before any Anglo-American units entered France – the Red Army moved over the Polish border. Italy was already in the process of occupation. On 6 June 1944 came D-Day, when the cross-Channel invasion was finally launched, thus engaging the main German Army on two fronts. However, as military victories increased, political difficulties also began to impinge. With the liberation of Eastern Europe by the Red Army alone, questions about post-war boundaries and political developments came to the fore. FDR had deliberately sought to concentrate upon victory and the unconditional surrender of the Axis powers, goals on which the disparate members of the Alliance could agree. As Soviet troops liberated Poland, Rumania, Hungary and Bulgaria, pro-Soviet groups were encouraged and economic reparations were exacted, and fears grew as to Stalin's ultimate intentions. In Italy, meanwhile, the occupation remained in the control of the United States and Great Britain. On the other side of the world, the Pacific War continued, but it became increasingly apparent that the Chinese Nationalist leader, Chiang Kai-Shek, was so preoccupied by civil war that he would be unable to make a major contribution to the liberation of the Far East. With the certainty that the Japanese defence would be prolonged and bitter, the need for extra manpower from the Soviet Union – which had not yet declared war upon Japan – became paramount.

Thus, as the war progressed, the number of issues requiring discussion between the Allies increased. It was necessary to decide upon the overall strategic priorities, on which the British, Americans and Russians rarely all shared the same goals. Moreover, such matters as the policy to be followed towards the liberated areas of Europe, the treatment to be meted out to the Axis powers once they were defeated, and the wider issue of post-war reconstruction and planning were the subjects of discord. Inevitably, there were major differences of opinion between the world's leading capitalist nation, the world's leading communist regime and the world's largest empire. Yet in discussing these issues, Roosevelt was handicapped by his inability to delegate decision-making powers. The President kept his cards close to his chest and the shape of his overall policy was far from clear. Harry Hopkins was privy to the president's opinions, but he was merely the Secretary of Commerce and therefore ill-placed to take part in any formal conference. Hence, the solution was found in a series of wartime conferences between Roosevelt himself and either Winston Churchill alone or, on a number of occasions, both the main Allied leaders. In addition to a number of meetings in Canada or the United States, Churchill and Roosevelt met at Casablanca in January 1943 and Cairo in November 1943. Both men met with Stalin in the Iranian capital of Teheran, immediately after their Cairo conference, and at Yalta, in the Crimea, during February 1945. These meetings offered a chance for face-to-face bargaining and joint policy formation; without them suspicion would undoubtedly have been greater and the reaching of agreement on key strategic decisions considerably handicapped.

These unprecedented wartime summits – Roosevelt was the first American president to leave the United States during wartime and only the second to leave the hemisphere during his term of office – fitted in well with his reliance upon personal contact, conversation and persuasion. The relationship between Roosevelt and the other two leaders was ostensibly very good – in contrast to the relationship between Churchill and Stalin, which was guarded and reflected Churchill's personal antipathy for Bolshevism. The unity thus created between the 'Big Three' was of great importance and was, to a very large degree, the personal creation of Roosevelt. The President shrewdly recognized the critical importance of 'Uncle Joe'

Stalin to the Soviet war effort, and utilized all his personal charm to win over the Soviet leader. Pointed jokes made at Churchill's expense played a large part in breaking the ice. With Churchill too there was a careful nurturing of relationships. The exchange of letters and telegrams between 'POTUS' (President of the United States) and 'Former Naval Person' (Prime Minister Churchill), even before the United States entered the war, helped form a strong bond between the two men. Both were at pains to exchange personal greetings and small gifts, thus emphasizing their good working relationship. FDR responded to a birthday greeting from Churchill with the comment that 'it is great fun to be in the same decade with you', and at the height of the war wistfully wrote, 'some day I hope you will get enough time to resume the painting and that I will be able to return to making ship models and collecting stamps!'[1]

By building up a relationship with both Stalin and Churchill, the president was able to act as a mediator on several occasions, aided by the fact that he presided over the meetings, since of the three, he was the only head of state. However, Roosevelt's reliance upon his own personal diplomacy and his unwillingness to involve Vice-President Truman in the closing months of his adminis- tration had adverse consequences. Accusations have been made that Roosevelt allowed himself to be beguiled by Stalin, to the cost of Eastern Europe; while following his death, neither the State Department nor the new president were fully *au fait* with the complex inter- national situation. It would however be wrong to assume that in order to preserve harmony, FDR accepted wholeheartedly the views of his allies. Both of course, had their own strong objectives, which in many cases clashed with American ideals. Churchill was devoted to the preservation of the British Empire, for example, whilst Stalin was determined to erect a buffer zone of Eastern European states closely linked to the Soviet Union both politically and economically.

It was partly to avoid disagreements on such matters that FDR sought to postpone the evolution of concrete post-war plans for as long as possible. Even so, he was often perturbed by what he saw as British attempts to direct Allied strategy in such a way as to best serve the preservation of the British Empire. He clashed with Churchill on many occasions over colonial policy, and particularly the future of India. FDR believed that imperial rule simply perpetuated underdevelopment and often he emphasized the importance of self-determination – views which did not find much favour with Churchill. The President attempted to find some alternative for French colonies in the Far East, such as United Nations trusteeships, efforts which aroused considerable British opposition and which were eventually abortive. As the end of the war approached, differences occurred on a number of issues, including plans for post-war civil aviation, the future of Lend Lease, policy towards Greece in late 1944 and the line to be taken about Russian policy in Poland.

There are also signs that, despite his earlier *bonhomie* towards Stalin, Roosevelt's suspicions of Soviet intentions were growing during 1944. The strong China that he hoped to promote would act as a counter to Russian power in the Far East. In September 1944 FDR and Churchill decided specifically that the USSR would not be admitted to a share in the control and use of atomic energy. However, the paramount need was to maintain the Soviet contribution to the war effort and therefore too firm a stance could not be adopted. In foreign policy, as in domestic affairs, Roosevelt had a strong sense of realism, and understood the need to take account of what was achievable, not just what was desirable. Yet his dreams of the United Nations (UN) were based upon an assumption of superpower co-operation, not conflict, suggesting an idealistic core to his thinking which he was reluctant totally to abandon.

The wartime meetings of the Big Three reflected these

two strains in Roosevelt's thinking; the desire to maintain Allied unity, yet suspicion of both British and Soviet intentions in a number of areas. It was in post-war planning, rather than military strategy, that many of the differences lay – with the exception of the issue of the Second Front, which was finally decided at Teheran in December 1943. At that meeting, the main emphasis was upon the fighting of the war, although Roosevelt raised the question of a collective security organization, to be called the United Nations Organization. His own preference was for a structure which would place most power in the hands of 'Four Policemen' – the United States, the Soviet Union, Great Britain and China, all of which would assume regional peacekeeping responsibilities. Domestic pressure forced him to adopt a more multilateral approach to the question of collective security. Nonetheless, the composition and power of the Security Council with its five permanent members, made plain that the UN was to be more hierarchical than had been the League. Once the Big Three had agreed to the concept of the UN, concrete steps could be taken to plan its structure, culminating in the Dumbarton Oaks conference in Washington D.C. during 1944. Also at Teheran it was decided that Germany and Japan would need to be tightly controlled after the war, possibly by territorial division. It was also agreed that the Soviet Union should retain control of the Baltic States and would make some gains in Polish territory, thus meeting some of the Soviet goals as regards security. However, the question of post-war Poland was left somewhat vague, as FDR was anxious not to alienate Polish-Americans close to the 1944 election.

During 1944, there was no meeting of the Big Three, although a number of important political issues began to arise. In the Far East Roosevelt wished to see the emergence of a strong China to act as a policeman in the region, together with the elimination of the French Empire. Both of these goals were to be undermined;

Chiang Kai-Shek lacked the authority, efficiency or will to play a major part in international affairs, while in the case of Indochina early hopes of a trusteeship had to bow to fears of Soviet influence and political instability – and British insistence. Roosevelt's determined backing for Chiang Kai-Shek and his evident dislike of de Gaulle, were both errors of judgement in terms of post-war power politics. The problems of reconciling wartime co-operation and victory with post-war security and control of both Germany and the Soviet Union proved an immense problem. Part of the dilemma was that public pressure to withdraw American troops from Europe immediately war was over seemed very likely. The UN would provide a forum to discuss disputes, but this still left the problem of post-war boundaries and the setting-up of governments in the newly liberated territories behind the advancing Red Army. By the time the three leaders next met, at Yalta in the Crimea, it was February 1945 and the end of the war in Europe was in sight.

At Yalta, then, two questions were pressing; the need to secure Russian agreement to entering the Far Eastern war; and the political future of Eastern Europe, which had been liberated by the Red Army. On the first, Stalin agreed to enter the war against Japan by no later than three months after victory in Europe, in return for substantial territorial concessions in the Far East. This was FDR's key aim and he was immensely relieved to have secured this. The prevailing assumption was that the war against Japan could be expected to continue for at least another year to eighteen months and that the fighting would be particularly intense. Roosevelt, anxious to limit American casualties and aware that the Chinese government forces were unlikely to play any major part, hoped to enlist the assistance of Russian troops. On the second matter – that of the fate of Eastern Europe – there were vaguely worded agreements concerning the composition of the new Polish government, the setting-up of democratic governments in Eastern Europe and the holding of free elections. The three powers agreed to a Declaration of Liberated Europe, but no machinery was established for ensuring that these commitments were honoured.

It has been commented that the Yalta agreement on Eastern Europe was so elastic that it could be stretched to mean whatever Stalin wanted. This has led some historians to blame FDR for 'giving away' Eastern Europe to the Soviets, as a result of his own failing health and his naive acceptance of Stalin's evasive promises. Thus, it can be argued, Roosevelt helped set the scene for the Cold War. However, there was little that Roosevelt could gain by insisting upon watertight agreements on 'free elections' and 'democratic governments' – even assuming that common ground could be found between the United States and the Soviet Union on what those two terms meant – whilst there was much to lose, including the use of the Red Army in the Far East. In short, at Yalta Roosevelt did no more than recognize realities; to argue that he 'gave away' Eastern Europe is to assume that it was his to give away. Cold logic – the logic of an occupying Red Army – dictated that Stalin would have a pre-eminent voice in the settlement of Eastern Europe. Short of outright war against the Soviets, the Western powers could do little more than acquiesce. And with the war in the Pacific still to be won, the alienation of Stalin was not to be lightly undertaken. Roosevelt himself did not claim that he had gained all that he had hoped from Yalta; it was however, he commented, 'the best that I could do'.[2] There was quite simply no way that Roosevelt could afford to take a hard line with Stalin, even if he had hopes of prevailing in the face of Soviet obsession with national security.

Within only a few months Roosevelt's successor, Harry Truman, was to take a very hard line against the Soviets. However, by then the atomic bomb had been successfully tested, and many American policy-makers believed that the atomic monopoly changed dramatically the balance of power between East and West. Although it was under his successor that the bomb was first used, in August 1945, Roosevelt inaugurated the atomic age, in that he gave his support to the Manhattan Project and tried to ensure that its existence was kept a secret from the Soviets. Indeed, at one stage the Americans even sought to exclude the British from its control and development, although at the insistence of Churchill this decision was reversed. Given reports that the Germans were also engaged upon the development of atomic weapons, it is hardly surprising that the Allies too were keen to harness the power of the atom. Whilst the sheer destructive capacity of the bomb was not recognized until a very late stage, it was apparent that this weapon would change the shape of international warfare. There is no reason to think that Roosevelt would have hesitated to use the weapon, once perfected. FDR's part in the shaping of the atomic age and the Cold War with which atomic diplomacy was intricately involved cannot be ignored; it is not accurate to assume that had he continued in the presidency, the Cold War would have been averted. However, neither is it appropriate to assume that FDR foresaw the consequences of the steps he took, under wartime conditions, to develop new weapons and to avoid irremediable conflict with a key ally.

Roosevelt's contribution to wartime strategy and post-war planning was thus a considerable one. As his confidence grew, he became more assertive in his relations with the other major Allied powers and was able to secure many of his objectives. Yet in evolving his policies, FDR was very much led by events, rather than by a compelling and coherent policy structure. His shifts in opinion and emphasis, his slowness to evolve specific wartime aims, made it difficult for others to act on his behalf. Moreover, his foreign policy had also to take account of internal developments within the United States. It must not be forgotten that at the same time as fulfilling his international responsibilities, Roosevelt was also responsible for the domestic policy followed by the US Government. An important aspect of this was the mobilization of the economy to meet the needs of war. To do this, he was prepared to put behind him some of the preconceptions and opinions shaped during earlier years; as he himself put it in December 1943, 'Dr New Deal' was replaced by 'Dr Win the War'.

Thus, the anti-trust campaign against business was largely suspended, as in a number of instances the Justice Department was preparing to bring cases against companies vital to the war effort. Businessmen were pressed into service to run the myriad wartime agencies concerned with production and supply, such as the War Production Board, the Office of Economic Stabilization, the War Labour Board and a host of others. Roosevelt's skills remained much as they had been in the New Deal; as Frances Perkins put it, 'He was a creative and energizing agent rather than a careful, direct-line administrator.'[3] Several New Deal agencies, among them the CCC, the NYA and the WPA, were wound up during the war. Washington in the war years, therefore, was rather more conservative than in the 1930s. There were less positive aspects of the domestic scene, such as the decision by the administration to move over 100,000 Japanese–Americans, many of them American citizens born in the United States, to inland camps, on the basis that they were all potential fifth columnists. This blatant infringement of civil liberties had FDR's personal concurrence. In domestic as well as international affairs, therefore, FDR demonstrated his capacity to respond to events, sometimes in contradiction to his principles.

However, FDR had not completely abandoned his reformist aims, even if much of his reform zeal was diverted to international concerns, such as anti-imperialism and collective security. He devoted a lot of time and attention to building up domestic support for the UN, so as to avoid a repetition of 1920. He addressed this at two levels. In practical terms, he sought to relieve American fears that the UN might be able to commit American troops to war without the direct consent of congress. Thus, much was made of the veto power held by the members of the Security Council. Even so, FDR made it plain that he expected the UN to exercise powers of rapid response to emergencies. In his usual homely attempt to find an everyday analogy, he commented that he did not wish to create the kind of situation where a policeman who saw a felon break into a house had to go to the Town Hall and call a town meeting to issue a warrant before the felon could be arrested. On a more inspirational level, he exhorted his fellow countrymen not to repeat their earlier mistakes. Three months before his death, in his State of the Union address, he urged: 'In our disillusionment after the first war, we gave up the hope of achieving a better peace because we had not the courage to fulfil our responsibilities in an admittedly imperfect world. We must not let that happen again, or we shall follow the same tragic road again – the road to a third world war.'[4]

In addition, as the war progressed, a feeling of apathy and uncertainty on the home front required some action on the part of the federal government – particularly if the Democrats were to retain hold of the federal government. In the mid-term elections of 1942, the Republicans had made substantial gains, only narrowly failing to secure control of the House of Representatives. So the President returned to domestic reform, seeking to assure Americans that the war would have positive conse- quences at home as well as abroad. In January 1944 he used his State of the Union message to promote the notion of a Second Bill of Rights, intended to tackle the question of economic rights, and based upon the asser- tion that Americans had economic and social rights, including the right to employment at adequate wages, a competitive business environment, a decent home, adequate medical care, a welfare system and a good education. However, nothing was done actually to put these 'rights' into practice. Roosevelt was however able to implement a major programme of benefits for ex-servicemen, including education opportunities, health benefits and home loans.

Ironically, the war was to achieve much of what the New Deal had failed to accomplish. Prosperity and afflu-ence returned, with virtually the end of unemployment and a booming productive capacity which left the United States head and shoulders above the rest of the world's economies. Untouched by the actual fighting, productive plant remained intact and the workforce increased its skills as women were trained to take the places of men at the front. Wages and the standard of living rose. The powers of government expanded enormously, with the power to allocate priorities, organize production and direct labour. The government became a major consumer as defence contracts mushroomed. In order to meet the costs, deficit spending increased, and the national debt rose from under $50 billion in 1941 to over $250 billion in 1945. Even so, the base of the tax-paying pyramid increased, with over 40 million families paying income tax in 1944 compared with only four million in 1939. In the field of race relations, there were some concessions to blacks, but they were of limited scope and granted only reluctantly. In the face of strong pressure from blacks, FDR did issue orders preventing discrimination on the grounds of colour, race or creed in the defence industries and set up a Fair Employment Practices Committee. Nonetheless, the armed services remained segregated throughout the war.

Roosevelt also had to contend with a presidential elec-tion in the midst of war. Whereas the British had suspended the normal electoral processes during the war, in the USA elections took place as normal in 1942 and 1944. The vexed question was, obviously, whether FDR would run in November 1944. Having once broken the two-term precedent, it was somewhat easier for him to run yet again. By now, he had probably come to believe that no one else could take over the running of the wartime effort, and to some extent, this was true. He was, however, slow to admit that he would be a candidate. Finally, in July 1944 he wrote to the National Democratic Party Chairman, Robert Hannegan, stating that he would prefer to return to Hyde Park, but if called upon to do so he would run again. He compared himself, as Commander-in-Chief, to a soldier who had a duty to serve in whatever capacity required by the American people. However, he did not really enter the campaign actively until its closing stages, when he was stung by the charges and innuendoes of his opponent, Tom Dewey, into a short but intense burst of activity. The opening of his campaign came on 23 September, when he made a speech at a Teamsters Union banquet in Washington D.C., using his braces for the first time in a long while to emphasize his physical capability. The election results were again a mandate for Roosevelt, although his margin of victory in terms of the popular vote was the narrowest of all his four elections. Roosevelt again changed his running mate however. He had in fact done little to groom a successor within the Democratic party. Those whom he could trust to safeguard the New Deal, such as Harry Hopkins, did not necessarily have the necessary support from the party hierarchy. Conversely, party stalwarts such as Jim Farley were rarely devoted New Dealers. His eventual vice-presidential running mate, Harry Truman, was not his first choice, but as a popular senator might well be in a good position to manipulate the Senate vote when it came to the ratification of the UN, while Henry Wallace had not been particularly effective in his years as chairman of the Senate.

Following his victory in 1944, FDR was inaugurated as President of the United States for the fourth time on 20 January 1945. As an economy measure, he took the oath of office not at the Capitol, but on the South Portico of the White House. His inaugural address was short and the traditional parades were abandoned. Although this was appropriate to the wartime setting, it also eased the strain upon the President, whose health was beginning to fail. He was to serve less than three months of his fourth term, before his death in office on 12 April 1945. During that time, despite concerns about his health, he had made an exhausting trip to Yalta, in order to meet his fellow Allied leaders. Inevitably, given the death of FDR in office so soon after his fourth inaugural, speculation has centred upon his health. Was FDR a dying man when he went to Yalta? Was he unfit to run for office again in 1944, but misled by his doctors? Historian Jim Bishop has written a lengthy account of his final year of life, concluding that FDR was a dying man even before his re-election, but that his true condition was hidden from him by his doctors – an account denied by two of his sons. In his last year, FDR was suffering from an enlarged heart, a hardening of the arteries, hypertension and chronic fatigue; not that uncommon for a man in his sixties, perhaps, but Roosevelt had also to contend with the strain of disability and the tensions and stress of high office.

The strain of twelve years in the Presidency obviously took their toll of FDR, especially as so many of them were preoccupied with crisis. There were clear signs that he was becoming more intolerant, less willing to compromise. It must also be remembered that he had few real friends. His wife was growing increasingly apart from him, as they both developed different interests and travelled independently. Eleanor also had a busy schedule of visits, including foreign trips to visit American servicemen. Hopkins was less frequently at his side, as a result of first his marriage and then his illness. FDR's faithful secretary, Missy LeHand, fell seriously ill and died in 1941. His secretary and aide, 'Pa' Watson, died on board ship while returning from Yalta. Thus, during his last four years at the White House, FDR led an increasingly isolated existence. His sons were in uniform and at home far less often, although occasionally one was deputed to act as aide on his foreign trips. Wartime security arrangements were necessarily increased, while Roosevelt's own physical disability made mobility difficult even on a day-to day basis.

On the other hand, Roosevelt did use wartime secrecy as an opportunity to visit Warm Springs and Hyde Park more frequently. Although he was lonely in the closing years of his life, he had rarely made close friendships during his public life, instead relying upon confidantes and aides. He did, however, renew one old acquaintance. In his closing years, FDR again met Lucy Mercer Rutherford, the woman whom he had promised never to see again. In 1944 Lucy was widowed and this appears to have released the constraint upon their meeting. On trips to Georgia FDR occasionally detoured to meet Lucy; she was staying at Warm Springs and was in the same room as him when he had his fatal stroke. Yet much of the gaiety and enjoyment had left his life, even though very few contemporaries recognized the fact. He had built up and retained a façade, to the extent that very few saw the real man behind the famous smile, pince-nez and tilted cigarette holder.

Signs of the president's deteriorating health were apparent upon his return from Yalta. Photographs taken at the conference show a frail and aging man; he delivered his report upon the meeting to Congress whilst sitting down, a rare concession to his physical disability. Even more poignantly, his superb speech delivery, upon which so much of his political appeal was based, was showing signs of disarray, as he slurred and stumbled over his words. Yet, whilst such outward manifestations of weakness shocked immediate observers, news of his death from a massive brain haemorrhage, while on vacation in Warm Springs, took the country by surprise. The death of the man who had steered his country through the two worst crises of the 20th century came as an immense shock. Many could not really remember any president other than Roosevelt. The slow journey of his body from Georgia to Washington D.C. became the focus of an immense display of personal grief as thousands gathered to see the train carrying his coffin go by. After a short memorial service in the White House, Roosevelt made his final journey to his beloved Hyde Park, where, as he had requested, on 15 April he was buried in his mother's rose garden, a short walk from the house where he had been born. Only a simple stone marks the grave of the 32nd President of the United States. His main gift to his country had been the restoration of America's faith in itself. 'The only limitation to our realization of tomorrow will be our doubts of today. Let us move forward with strong and active faith.'[5]

Conclusion 7

Franklin Delano Roosevelt was President of the United States in a period almost unparalleled in its turbulence and uncertainty. The global depression and the international crises culminating in the Second World War profoundly altered the world. As he himself said, 'There is a mysterious cycle in human events. To some generations much is given. Of other generations much is expected. This generation of Americans has a rendezvous with destiny.'[1] So, too, did he. The greatest of all 20th-century presidents, he shaped the course not only of his own country's history, but also that of the world. The twelve years of his presidency saw transformations on an unparalleled scale. At home, the role of the federal government was revolutionized and the modern presidency was born. Abroad, the USA eventually accepted under FDR's guidance the role of leader of the Western world. Throughout it all, he retained and preached the belief in democracy and peace which provided the unifying force behind all his actions.

Within the USA, FDR's main achievement must undoubtedly be the initiation and implementation of the New Deal. Through its many programmes, through his fireside chats, through his reaching out to the American public, FDR made the presidency relevant to every inhabitant of the nation. It was now seen as the right and indeed the duty of the federal government to concern itself with matters of social welfare and economic planning. The extent to which the New Deal had revolutionized the American political agenda is demonstrated by the later acceptance of its main provisions by the Republican party, thus establishing a bipartisan consensus which lasted until the 1980s. Democratic presidents in the post-war era vied to offer programmes which built upon the New Deal's achievements – the Fair Deal, the New Frontier, the Great Society. The language, the methods and many of the goals were those of FDR, although later presidents also addressed the one area where Roosevelt had been conspicuously silent – that of civil rights. Whatever the limitations of the New Deal – and as Leuchtenberg has written, it was only 'a half-way revolution'[2] – it transformed the domestic politics of the USA.

This is despite the fact that, in terms of its response to the Depression, Roosevelt's administration was far from being a success economically. This is best illustrated by comparing the USA with Germany, the other country worst hit by the impact of the world depression. In the case of Germany, economic recovery was faster and more sustained than in the USA. Yet it was achieved at immense political and social cost. In the USA, on the other hand, economic recovery was slow, and subject to downturns – notably in 1937. Yet politically, the USA absorbed the pressures of crisis. FDR proved adept at recruiting the leaders and adopting the programmes of protest movements, so that discontent could express itself through existing mechanisms. The New Deal was far more of a political than an economic programme, a reflection perhaps of the fact that FDR was himself no economist.

Conclusion

Roosevelt was also responsible for major changes in the American political structure. He presided over the transformation of the Democratic party into a progressive–liberal coalition, with strong ties to organized labour and the working classes of the cities. The influence of white Southerners in the party still remained, but their conservative influence was considerably reduced. Even more significantly, he presided over the transformation of the office of president into a modern, adequately staffed executive, which initiated and implemented domestic programmes and enjoyed an enhanced power of direction in foreign affairs. Many of the New Deal measures delegated wide-ranging discretionary powers to the President, thus expanding the executive direction of policy. Roosevelt undoubtedly built upon the work of others, but the rise of the modern presidency is clearly identified with him. This was not an entirely unmixed blessing, as his terms in office also saw the beginnings of the 'imperial presidency'. But FDR left the office of the president in a far better state to take on the demands of the 20th century, demands that were to escalate in the Cold War years.

Roosevelt did not provide a carefully constructed ideology for his successors to pursue. He was a politician above all else, responding to political realities and accepting the consequent limitations upon his freedom of action. In his early years, at Groton and Harvard, Roosevelt learnt the attitudes and prejudices of a gentleman; through his upbringing and probably most of all as a result of his polio attack, he developed a strong humanitarianism. His faith in God was a direct and simple one, and strongly influenced his own behaviour and attitudes, not least his self-confidence and assurance in the face of all crises. He himself, when once asked his philosophy, stated, 'My philosophy? I am a Christian and a Democrat.'[3] Biographers have found it extraordinarily hard to understand Roosevelt. It is difficult to fathom his own views and ideas: he kept no diary, his correspondence, though lively and outgoing, was tailored to its recipient and he had no really close personal friend to whom he could express his ideas unreservedly. One reason why the New Deal appears so evasive is that there was no coherent philosophy behind it. A frequent comment by historians such as Conkin and Burns is that FDR operated mostly at the level of unarticulated – and possibly intuitive – beliefs. Yet he would have been far less effective had he dogmatically sought to implement a specific programme. For Roosevelt's skill as a leader in times of crisis went beyond the effects of any specific, coherent programme. He established a dialogue with the American people and restored their trust, confidence and faith. He had a gift of simplification; even if he was not a great orator in the grand style, he was a marvellous communicator.

It was not only in the domestic sphere that Franklin Roosevelt was responsible for major changes and achievements, but also in the international arena. He thus stands out amongst American presidents, few of whom have had so decisive an influence in both domestic and foreign policy. What, then, did he achieve abroad? His main goal, and the one which he failed to implement, was peace – peace for the United States in the first instance, but also on a global level. He fought desperately to protect the Americas from the spreading international crisis, but without success. The growing tension in Europe was apparent long before September 1939, thus giving international statesmen like President Roosevelt the opportunity – if they chose to exercise it – to try to influence events. FDR did not so choose. After 1939, he supported democracy on the international scene, as he pursued it at home, but desperately hoped to protect his country from war. And yet, once the die was cast by Pearl Harbor, he proved to be an extraordinary war leader, who did much to shape the course of the war and the nature of the peace. This is not to say that the results were always beneficial. But although he died before peace was declared, the post-war world owed much to FDR. His commitment to the UN was clear, as was his belief that the USA must be prepared to play a significant part in the post-war organization of the world. His strong anti-imperialism, his commitment to democracy, although in some ways naive and unrealistic, permeated not only the rhetoric, but also some of the action, of the wartime alliance. He recognized, and made the American people recognize, that their national security could only be secured at the global level. Although he could not have prevented the wartime alliance souring into Cold War tension, his death in the critical closing stages of the war was a tragedy for the world.

The relationship which FDR formed with Churchill, though conducted more by correspondence than face to face, and having within it immense strains and tensions, was nonetheless an important one for both men. It fell to Churchill to pay a tribute to the late President in the House of Commons only days after his death; and as a master of rhetoric, he summed up much of what made FDR so powerful a figure within the century. 'His love of his own country, his respect for its constitution, his power of gauging the tides and currents of its mobile public opinions, were always evident, but added to these were the beatings of that generous heart which was always stirred to anger and to action by spectacles of aggression and oppression by the strong against the weak.'[4] Both at home, in the Depression-torn United States, and ultimately abroad, in the face of fascist aggression, President Franklin Delano Roosevelt stood up for the weak, and in so doing, profoundly changed the world he left behind him.

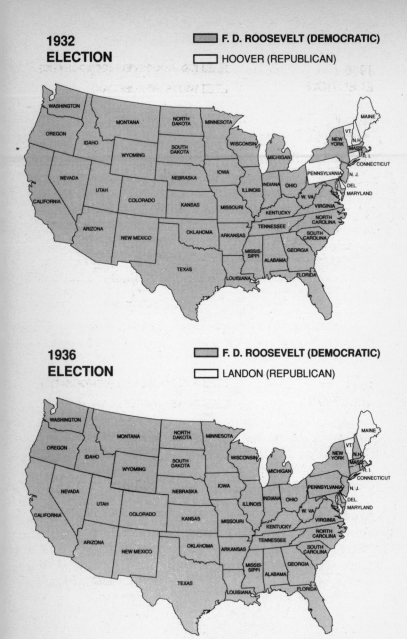

1932 ELECTION

F. D. ROOSEVELT (DEMOCRATIC)

HOOVER (REPUBLICAN)

1936 ELECTION

F. D. ROOSEVELT (DEMOCRATIC)

LANDON (REPUBLICAN)

Maps showing Electoral Votes by States, Presidential Elections 1932–44

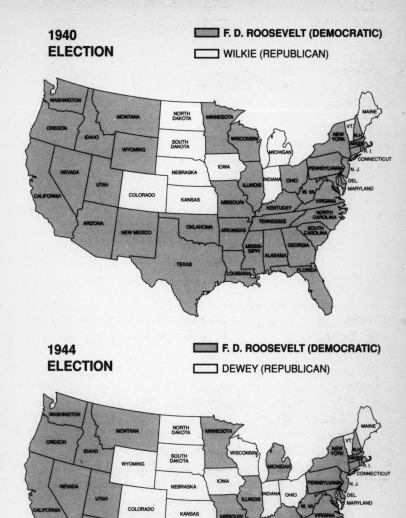

1940 ELECTION

▨ F. D. ROOSEVELT (DEMOCRATIC)
☐ WILKIE (REPUBLICAN)

1944 ELECTION

▨ F. D. ROOSEVELT (DEMOCRATIC)
☐ DEWEY (REPUBLICAN)

References

Chapter 1

1. See 'Select Bibliography' for more details upon individual interpretations of FDR's historical significance.
2. James Roosevelt (with Bill Liddy), *My Parents: A Differing View*, W.H. Allen: London, 1977, p. 21.
3. Quoted by Ted Morgan, *FDR: A Biography*, Simon and Schuster: New York, 1985, p. 166.
4. Hugh Gregory Gallagher, *FDR's Splendid Deception*, Dodd, Mead and Co: New York, 1985, p. xi. This book, written by a polio sufferer, is the most comprehensive study of FDR's physical disability.
5. A key example of this is given by Ted Morgan, *op. cit.*, pp. 258–62 and 771. See also Frances Perkins, *The Roosevelt I Knew*, Hamish Hamilton: London, 1947, pp. 29–30.

Chapter 2

1. He was officially out of office, although President-elect, from January to 4 March 1933.

2. FDR message to New York legislature, 28 August 1931, in S.I. Rosenman (ed.), *The Public Papers and Addresses of Franklin D. Roosevelt 1928-45*, 13 vols, Random House: New York, 1938–1950, [hereafter *Roosevelt Papers*, plus volume] I, p. 458.

3. Frank B. Freidel, *Franklin D. Roosevelt: The Triumph*, Little, Brown and Co: Boston, 1956, pp. 248–9.

4. FDR speech, 7 April 1932, *Roosevelt Papers* I, p. 625.

5. FDR speech, 22 May 1932, *Roosevelt Papers* I, pp. 639–47.

6. FDR speech to the Democratic Party convention, 2 July 1932, *Roosevelt Papers* I, p. 659.

7. Joseph P. Lash, *Eleanor and Franklin: The Story of their Relationship, based on Eleanor Roosevelt's private papers*, André Deutsch: London, 1972, p. 339.

Chapter 3

1. One example of this is Arthur Schlesinger Jr, *The Age of Roosevelt*, 3 vols, Houghton Mifflin: Boston, 1956–60. See also Rexford Tugwell, *The Democratic Roosevelt*, Pelican: Baltimore, 1969.

2. First Inaugural Address, 4 March 1933, *Roosevelt Papers*, II, pp. 11–16.

3. Raymond Moley, *After Seven Years*, pp. 369–70, quoted in Leuchtenberg, *Franklin D. Roosevelt and the New Deal*, Harper and Row: New York, 1963, p. 33.

4. First Fireside Chat, 12 March 1933, *Roosevelt Papers*, II, pp. 61–5.

5. Studs Terkel, *Hard Times: An Oral History of the Great Depression*, Random House: New York, 1970, p. 115.

6. Fireside Chat, 28 June 1934, *Roosevelt Papers*, III, p. 314.

7. The other was Douglas MacArthur.

8. State of the Union message, 4 January 1935, *Roosevelt Papers*, IV, pp. 15–25.

9. Roosevelt press conference, 31 May 1935, *Roosevelt Papers*, IV, p. 221.

Chapter 4

1. Schlesinger, *op. cit.*, III, p. 392.
2. FDR Address at a Jackson Day Dinner, 8 January 1936, *Roosevelt Papers*, V, p. 43.
3. Schlesinger, *op. cit.*, II, p. 304.
4. Terkel, *op. cit.*, p. 135.
5. Speech by FDR, 31 October 1936, *Roosevelt Papers*, V, pp. 568–9.
6. Up to and including 1933, presidential terms had traditionally begun in the March following the November election. Congress had agreed in 1932 that, commencing in 1937, the presidential inauguration would he held in January.
7. Second Inaugural address, 20 January 1937, *Roosevelt Papers*, VI, pp. 1–6.
8. James MacGregor Burns, *The Lion and the Fox 1882–1940*, Harcourt Brace and World Inc: New York, 1956, p. vii.
9. Paul K. Conkin, *The New Deal*, Routledge and Kegan Paul: London, 1968, p. 73.
10. Both quotations come from Studs Terkel, *op. cit.*, pp. 34 and 86.

Chapter 5

1. Address at Chicago, 5 October 1937, *Roosevelt Papers*, VI, pp. 406–11.
2. Fireside Chat, 3 September 1939, *Roosevelt Papers*, VIII, pp. 460–4.
3. FDR speech, 10 June 1940, *Roosevelt Papers*, IX, p. 264.

4. FDR speech, 30 October 1940, *Roosevelt Papers* IX, p. 517.
5. Fireside Chat, 29 December 1940, *Roosevelt Papers* IX pp. 633–645.
6. See, as a classic example, Charles C. Tansill, *Back Door to War: The Roosevelt Foreign Policy, 1933–41*, Henry Regnery Co.: Chicago, 1952.
7. Fireside chat, 11 September 1941, *Roosevelt Papers* X, p. 390.
8. Address by FDR to Congress, 8 December 1941, *Roosevelt Papers* X, p. 514.
9. FDR to Churchill, 8 December 1941, Warren F. Kimball (ed.), *Churchill and Roosevelt: the Complete Correspondence*, 3 vols, Princeton University Press: Princeton, 1984, I, p. 283.

Chapter 6

1. FDR to Churchill, 30 January 1942 and 11 February 1943, in Kimball, *op. cit.*, I, pp. 337 & 359.
2. Robert Dallek, *Franklin D. Roosevelt and American Foreign Policy, 1932–45*, Oxford University Press, New York: 1979, p. 521.
3. Perkins, *op. cit.*, p. 384.
4. FDR Speech, 6 January 1945, *Roosevelt Papers*, XIII, pp. 511–4.
5. Draft speech, *Roosevelt Papers*, XIII, p. 616. This quotation comes from a speech which he was preparing before his death, but which he never delivered.

Chapter 7

1. Speech by FDR, 17 June 1936, *Roosevelt Papers* V, p. 235.
2. Leuchtenberg, *op. cit.*, p. 347.

3. Schlesinger, *op. cit.*, II, p. 585.
4. Martin Gilbert, *Road to Victory: Winston S. Churchill 1941–45*, William Heinemann: London, 1986, p. 1301.

Select
Bibliography

There are several major biographies of Franklin Roosevelt available, not all of them complete. Ted Morgan, *FDR: A Biography* (Simon and Schuster: New York, 1985), stresses his weaknesses, while acknowledging his strengths. James McGregor Burns, *Roosevelt: The Lion and the Fox 1882–1940* (Harcourt Brace: New York, 1956) and *Roosevelt: The Soldier of Freedom 1940–45* (Weidenfeld and Nicolson: London, 1971), provides a thoughtful exploration of Roosevelt's leadership abilities and political goals. Frank B. Freidel, *Franklin D. Roosevelt*, 4 vols (Little, Brown and Co: Boston, 1952–73), is an extremely detailed study of the period until the end of 1933. Another multi-volume biography, still in progress, is Kenneth S. Davis, *FDR*, 3 vols (Random House: New York, 1972–86), which has so far reached 1937. A perceptive study of Roosevelt's early years is given by Geoffrey C. Ward, *Before the Trumpet: Young Franklin Roosevelt 1882–1905* (Harper and Row: New York, 1985). Joseph P. Lash, *Eleanor and Franklin: The Story of their Relationship* (André Deutsch: London, 1972), is a study of the Roosevelt marriage, written by a protégé of Eleanor Roosevelt. FDR did not himself write an autobiography, but Eleanor wrote a number of books, including two that are autobiographical, *This is My Story* (Harper and Brothers: New York, 1937), and *This I Remember* (Harper and Row: New York, 1949). Two of his sons also provided fascinating, if biased views of their father's life and opinions: James Roosevelt (with Bill Liddy), *My Parents: a Differing View* (W.H. Allen: London, 1977); and Elliott Roosevelt and James Brough, *A Rendezvous with Destiny: the Roosevelts of the White House* (W.H. Allen: London, 1977). The latter also produced a multi-volume collection of his father's personal correspondence, Elliott Roosevelt (ed.), *FDR: His Personal Letters*, 3 vols (Duell, Sloan and Pierce: New York, 1948). S.I. Rosenman (ed.), *The Public Papers and Addresses of Franklin D. Roosevelt 1928–1945*, 13 vols (Random House: New York, 1938–50), is a marvellous source for Roosevelt's own speeches.

On the New Deal years, there are a number of unusually helpful memoirs, although due account still has to be taken of the author's own prejudices. Rexford Tugwell wrote a work more akin to a biography than a personal memoir, *The Democratic Roosevelt* (Pelican: Baltimore, 1969). More critical appraisals are given by Raymond Moley, *After Seven Years* (Harper and Brothers: New York 1939), and by FDR's political manager, James A. Farley, *Jim Farley's Story* (Whittlesey House: New York, 1948). For an emphasis upon his social policy, see Frances Perkins, *The Roosevelt I Knew* (Hamish Hamilton: London, 1947). There are two excellent one-volume studies of the New Deal. The classic study is by William E. Leuchtenburg, *Franklin D. Roosevelt and the New Deal 1932–40* (Harper and Row: New York, 1963). Anthony Badger's work, *The New Deal: the Depression Years, 1933–1940* (Macmillan: London, 1989), does not place much stress upon FDR's contribution to the New Deal. Arthur Schlesinger Jr's study of the New Deal is incomplete, but emphasizes its positive, reforming aspects and its contribution to liberalism; he also stresses the division into two New Deals: Arthur M. Schlesinger, *The Age of Roosevelt*, 3 vols (Houghton Mifflin: Boston, 1956–1960). Far more critical of the New Deal is Paul Conkin, *The New Deal* (Routledge and Kegan Paul: London, 1968). However, most radical critiques of the New Deal have been published in article rather than monograph form.

On Roosevelt's foreign policy, the most detailed and judicious study is Robert Dallek, *Franklin D. Roosevelt and American Foreign Policy, 1932-45* (Oxford University Press: New York, 1979). An overtly hostile interpretation is given by Frederick W. Merks III, *Wind Over Sand: The Diplomacy of Franklin Roosevelt* (The University of Georgia Press: London, 1988). There are a number of works by Robert Divine, including *The Illusion of Neutrality* (University of Chicago Press: Chicago, 1962), *The Reluctant Belligerent: American Entry into World War II, 1939-41* (Wiley: New York, 1965), and *Roosevelt and World War II* (Johns Hopkins University Press: Baltimore, 1969). Roosevelt's relationship with Churchill is admirably revealed in Warren F. Kimball, *Churchill and Roosevelt: the Complete Correspondence*, 3 vols (Princeton University Press: Princeton, 1984).

Index

Agricultural Adjustment Act, 40, 41, 44, 50, 56, 61
America First Committee, 86
Atlantic Charter 94–5, 103
atomic bomb, 112–13
atomic energy, 109

banking, 40, 45–6, 59
Battle of Guadalcanal, 105
Battle of Midway, 105
Berle, Adolf, 29, 32
'Big Three', 107–9
Bill of Rights, 115–16
Black, Hugo, 68
Blue Eagle campaign, 50
Borneo, 104
Brandeis, Louis, 67
Brazil, 81
Bureau of the Budget, 75

Cairo Conference, 107
Campobello Island, 4, 13
Casablanca Conference, 107
'cash and carry' provisions, 90, 93
Central America, 80–81
Central Intelligence Agency, 75
Cermak, Anton, 34
Chamberlain, Neville, 89
Chile, 81

China, 85, 95–6, 106, 110–11
Churchill, Winston, 93, 95, 99, 100, 103, 104, 105, 107, 108, 109, 113
Civil Works Administration, 51–2
Civilian Conservation Corps, 42, 44, 114
coal mining, 60
Cohen, Ben, 60
Cold War, 1, 112, 113
collective bargaining, 59, 70–71
Commission on the Stabilization of Employment, 26
Committee of Industrial Organization, 70, 71
Commonwealth Club, San Francisco, 32
conservation, 41, 42
Corcoran, Tom, 60
corporate tax, 61
Coughlin, Charles, 53
Cox, James, 12, 13
Cuba, 81
Cufflinks Club, 47

D-Day, 106
Daniels, Josephus, 10, 11–12, 82
Davis, John W., 15
de Gaulle, Charles, 111

Index

Delano, Sara *see* Roosevelt, Sara
Delano, Walter, 96
Democratic National Committee, 28
Democratic Party, 62–3
Depression, 17–18, 23, 24–7, 34, 99
destroyers-for-bases deal, 93
Dewey, Tom, 117
Dumbarton Oaks Conference, 110

Early, Stephen, 13
economic recession, 1937, 71–2
electricity, 41–2
Emergency Banking Bill, 40, 45
Emergency Relief Appropriation Act, 55
Executive Reorganization Act, 75

Fair Employment Practices Committee, 116
Fair Labour Standards Act, 61, 74
Farley, Jim, 29, 30, 31, 75, 117
Farm Tenant Act, 69, 73
Federal Deposit Insurance Corporation, 42
Federal Emergency Relief Administration (FERA), 42, 44, 50, 51
Federal Reserve, 59
fireside chats, 45, 52, 94, 122
Flynn, Ed, 29
foreign affairs, 78–89
Four Freedoms Speech, 94

Garner, John Nance, 30, 73
General Motors, 70
government spending cuts, 40
Greater Asia Co-Prosperity Sphere, 97
Greece, 109
Groton, 5
Guam, 96, 103
Guffey Bituminous Coal Conservation Act, 56
Guffey-Snyder Act, 60

Haiti, 79
Hannegan, Robert, 117

Harding, Warren, 13
Harvard, 5–6
Hearst, William Randolph, 80
Hitler, Adolf, 85, 89
Holding Companies Bill, 58
Home Owners' Loan Corporation, 42
Hoover, Herbert, 17, 24, 25–6, 31, 32, 33, 34, 43, 83
Hopkins, Harry, 27, 42, 47, 72, 75, 99, 102, 107, 117, 118
housing acts, 69, 73
Howe, Louis, 9, 10, 13, 15, 27, 28, 29, 30, 47, 48, 75
Hughes, Charles Evans, 68
Hull, Cordell, 78, 81, 82, 84, 102
Hyde Park, 4, 46, 48, 119, 120

Iceland, 98
Ickes, Harold, 38
industrial policy, 40–41
Italy, 106

Japan, 79, 85, 91, 96–8, 100, 111
Johnson, Hugh, 50

Kai-Shek, Chiang, 96, 106, 111
Knox, Frank, 91

La Follette, Philip, 52–3, 74
La Guardia, Fiorello, 53
Labour Non-Partisan League, 64, 71
Landon, Alfred, 64, 65
Latin America, 80–83
League of Nations, 29–30, 78, 79, 85, 89
LeHand, Missy, 13, 47, 48, 119
Lend-Lease, 93–5, 109
Lewis, John, 70
liberalism, 2
London Economic Conference, 51, 84
Long, Huey, 53, 62

McIntyre, Marvin, 13
Malaya, 104
Manchuria, 80, 85
Manhattan Project, 113

Mercer, Lucy, 11, 49, 119
Mexico, 82
Miami, 34
Moley, Raymond, 29, 33, 39, 43, 60, 84
Moses, Robert, 19
Moskowitz, Belle, 19
Mussolini, Benito, 85, 89

National Foundation for Infantile Paralysis, 48
National Industrial Recovery Act (NIRA), 40–41, 44, 52, 53, 55, 60, 70
National Labour Relations (Wagner) Bill, 57, 58, 67, 68, 70
National Progressives of America, 74
National Recovery Administration, 50
National Security Council, 75
Navy, Assistant Secretary of, 9–12
Neutrality Acts, 86–7, 90, 99
New Deal, 2, 25, 27, 30, 31, 32–3, 73, 75, 76–7, 116, 121–2
    achievements & limitations of, 61–2
    First, 1933–5, 36–46, 50–56
        declared unconstitutional, 55–6
    Second, 1935–8, 36, 57–61, 65–6
New York, 4, 12
    Governor of, 15–27; reforms of 20–24
New York State Senate, 8
Newfoundland meeting, 94–5, 99
Nicaragua, 79

Oglethorpe University, 30
O'Gorman, James A., 8
old age insurance, 54, 59, 60
Olson, Floyd, 52
Overlord, Operation, 105–6

Panama Canal, 81
Peabody, Rev. Endicott, 5
Pearl Harbor, 98

Perkins, Frances, 18, 19, 21, 23, 38, 54, 58, 70, 114
Philippines, 96, 103–4
Platt Amendment, 81
Poland, 109, 112
presidential elections
    1920, 12–13
    1924, 15
    1928, 16
    1932, 27–33, 80
    1936, 64–5
    1940, 92
    1944, 116–17
Prohibition, 39, 40
public works, 40–41, 44
Public Works Administration, 55

'quarantine' speech, 88

Raskob, John, 28, 31
Reconstruction Finance Corporation, 25, 44
relief programmes, 42, 51–2
Resettlement Administration, 55
Reuben James, 99–100
Revolving Pensions Scheme, 53, 58
Roosevelt, Anna Eleanor, 7
Roosevelt, Eleanor, 6–7, 11, 14–15, 18, 20, 22, 47, 48–9, 75, 118
Roosevelt, Franklin Delano
    affair with Lucy Mercer, 3, 11, 49
    ancestors, 4
    and the rich, 63–4
    assassination attempt, 34–5
    character of, 3–4
    childhood of, 4–5
    communication with ordinary people, 46
    death of, 118–20
    education of, 5–6
    marriage of, 6–7
    polio, 3, 13–14, 48
    vice-presidential candidate, 1920, 12–13
Roosevelt, James (father), 4–5, 6
Roosevelt, James (son), 6, 47

Roosevelt, Klaes Martenszen Van, 4
Roosevelt, Sara, 4, 7, 11, 14, 47
Roosevelt, Theodore, 3, 4, 7, 10, 12–13, 15, 61, 79
Rosenman, Sam, 29
Rural Electrification Administration, 42
Rutherford, Lucy Mercer *see* Mercer, Lucy

St Lawrence River, 22
San Francisco, 32
Schechter Poultry Corporation v. United States, 55
Securities Exchange Act, 50
Share our Wealth Scheme, 53, 58
Sheehan, William F., 8
Singapore, 104
Smith, Al, 11, 12, 15, 16, 19, 21, 28
Social Security, 54, 55, 57, 58, 59, 60, 66–7, 68
Soil Conservation & Domestic Allotment Act, 61
Soviet Union, 2, 83, 95, 97
Spanish Civil War, 85
Stalin, Joseph, 105, 106, 107, 108, 109, 111, 112
Stimson, Henry, 80, 91
strikes, 70, 71
Supreme Court, 55–6, 64, 66–9

Tammany, 8, 9, 11, 12, 16, 22
taxation, 58, 61
Teheran Conference, 105, 107, 110
Temporary Emergency Relief Administration, 26, 27
Temporary National Economic Committee, 74
Tennessee Valley Authority (TVA), 41–2

Tojo, General, 98
Topeka, Kansas, 33
Torch Offensive, 104
Townsend, Francis, 53
trade unions, 70–71
Tripartite Pact, 91
Truman, Harry, 1, 108, 112, 117
Tugwell, Rexford, 29, 32, 33, 39, 54, 60

unemployment insurance, 26, 27, 59, 60
unemployment relief, 42, 51–2
United Nations, 1, 109, 110, 115
Security Council, 115, 125

Wagner Act, 57, 58, 67, 68, 70
Wake Island, 96, 103
Wall Street crash, 17, 24
Wallace, Henry, 91, 117
war debts, 84
Warm Springs, Georgia, 14, 15, 48, 119, 120
Watson, 'Pa', 119
Wheeler, Burton, 68
Wilkie, Wendell, 92
Wilson, Woodrow, 9, 12, 61, 89
Foundation, 79
Woodin, William, 38
work relief, 54
Works Progress Administration (WPA), 54–5, 114
World Court, 86
World War I, 10–11, 86
World War II, 89–119
post-war planning, 110–13
US internal policy, 114–16

Yalta Conference, 107, 111–12, 118, 119, 120

All Cardinal books in this series are available from good bookshops, or can be ordered from the following address:

Sphere Books
Cash Sales Department
P.O. Box 11
Falmouth
Cornwall TR10 9EN.

Please send cheque or postal order (no currency), and allow 60p for postage and packing for the first book plus 25p for the second book and 15p for each additional book ordered up to a maximum charge of £1.90 in U.K.

B.F.P.O. customers please allow 60p for the first book, 25p for the second book plus 15p per copy for the next 7 books, thereafter 9p per book.

Overseas customers, including Eire, please allow £1.25 for postage and packing for the first book, 75p for the second book and 28p for each subsequent title ordered.

CARDINAL